# Checking the Banks

# Checking the Banks

### The Nuts and Bolts of Banking
### for People Who Want to Fix It

Tom Sgouros

Light Publications
Providence

*For my children—and yours.*

Edited by Mark Binder
Design consultation by Beth Hellman
Typeset with LATEX (memoir class)

ISBN 978-0-9824707-2-5
Library of Congress Control Number: 2013957030
Printed in the United States of America
10 9 8 7 6 5 4 3 2 1
1.42

contact the author: tom@checkingthebanks.com

Light Publications
PO Box 2462
Providence, RI 02906
www.lightpublications.com

# Contents

**Prologue**     **1**

**1  Why change the banks?**     **5**

**2  Bank accounting made simple(r)**     **15**
Bank accounting 101 . . . . . . . . . . . . . . . . . . . . 15
Example balance sheets . . . . . . . . . . . . . . . . . . 30
Leverage . . . . . . . . . . . . . . . . . . . . . . . . . . . 36
Alternatives to fractional reserve banking . . . . . . . . 38

**3  Bank operation made simple(r)**     **41**
Bank income . . . . . . . . . . . . . . . . . . . . . . . . 42
Managing bank risk . . . . . . . . . . . . . . . . . . . . 45
Lending . . . . . . . . . . . . . . . . . . . . . . . . . . . 49
Borrowing . . . . . . . . . . . . . . . . . . . . . . . . . 58
The banking universe . . . . . . . . . . . . . . . . . . . 67
Payments . . . . . . . . . . . . . . . . . . . . . . . . . . 75
Where are the magic beans? . . . . . . . . . . . . . . . . 83

**4  Bank regulation**     **87**
Who are the regulators? . . . . . . . . . . . . . . . . . . 88
Federal Deposit Insurance Corporation . . . . . . . . . . 92
Evaluating and modeling risk . . . . . . . . . . . . . . . 94
Off-balance sheet activity . . . . . . . . . . . . . . . . . 98
The shadow banks . . . . . . . . . . . . . . . . . . . . . 101
Information asymmetry . . . . . . . . . . . . . . . . . . 103

**5  Starting a bank**     **105**
Early decisions . . . . . . . . . . . . . . . . . . . . . . . 107

Thinking like a banker . . . . . . . . . . . . . . . . . . . . . 108
What does a bank do with its capital? . . . . . . . . . . . 109
Making a bank's business plan . . . . . . . . . . . . . . 110
Financial projections . . . . . . . . . . . . . . . . . . . . . 113

**6 Basic government finance**     **117**
Budgets and financial reports . . . . . . . . . . . . . . . 119
Pension funds . . . . . . . . . . . . . . . . . . . . . . . . . 125
Government banking . . . . . . . . . . . . . . . . . . . . . 126
Bonds and other borrowing . . . . . . . . . . . . . . . . 128
Predatory public finance . . . . . . . . . . . . . . . . . . 137

**7 Potential banking scenarios**     **145**
Mutual banks and credit unions . . . . . . . . . . . . . 145
Public banks . . . . . . . . . . . . . . . . . . . . . . . . . . 147

**8 Epilogue**     **159**

**Further reading**     **163**

**Acknowledgments**     **165**

**Glossary**     **167**

**Index**     **197**

# Prologue: Banking for people who think banking is broken

THIS BOOK IS A ROUGH INTRODUCTION to a number of banking concepts useful to people who are dissatisfied with the current state of the banking industry in America. One of the common problems activists face is that they are, almost by definition, dilettantes. People who spend their careers studying banking tend to be, you'll be surprised to hear, bankers. By and large, they're happy with the system. And they should be; it's theirs. But the rest of us depend on it, and it does not serve us nearly so well.

Unfortunately, most of us spend our time in other occupations, acquiring other expertise. Some of us build things, some of us write things, and some of us simply learn how to be good humans. Which is all great, but it becomes a disadvantage when we notice that banks are messing things up for everyone and we don't have the vocabulary to discuss the problems with confidence. Worse, when discussing banking in public, the moment bankers turn to jargon, people who can't translate run for cover. This does nothing for their credibility, and basically slows down the whole process of fixing a broken system.

I earn my living in Rhode Island, as a freelance writer, engineer, and policy researcher, spending a lot of time on economics, taxation, finance, and other equally nerdy topics. In January of 1991, the new Governor of Rhode Island—only moments after being sworn in—was forced to declare a bank holiday and close 45 small banks and credit unions whose deposits had been insured by a private company. That company, owned and run by the very banks it supposedly regulated, turned out to be little more than a

1

nest of backslapping and incompetence, and was driven into sudden insolvency by spectacular misconduct at several of its member banks.[1] About a third of the state's population (including me) saw their bank accounts frozen and suddenly inaccessible. The debacle cost the state government over a billion dollars (a third of the annual budget at the time) and devastated the local economy. Trying to understand the problem, and then trying to imagine better policy responses than the ones on offer, began my career as a banking analyst.

Since then, I've helped dozens of elected officials understand how public finance really works, and created alternative banking proposals for activists and officials in Rhode Island and other states. Along the way I've felt the lack of a short and non-threatening introduction to banking, a companion I could trust to help me puzzle through reports and memos, and help me to have productive discussions on the subject with activists, bankers, regulators, and other government officials. I never did find a book like that, but instead found myself consulting banking text-books, technical reports, and academic papers, as well as harassing bankers of my acquaintance. It has been an effective education, but not the most efficient. This book is my attempt to mark the path I followed so that others can find their way along it more quickly than I did.

Here, then, is a modest list of useful concepts, a discussion of how banks work, and how they fail, as well as some suggestions for new institutions that might help make change. Faced with a landscape of unaccountable and damaging financial institutions, one sensible response is to attempt to regulate them better. Another is to invent new ones. Many people are working on the first response, with what one might charitably call mixed success. It's time for more people to take up the second.

Because some of the most intriguing possibilities for new institutions have to do with government and public control of finance, there is also some attention paid here to governments and their finances, with an eye to how the collective financial clout already contained in our nation's cities, counties, and states might be used to begin to rein in some of the excesses of the banking industry.

---

[1]This involved breathtaking embezzlement at two of the banks (see footnote on page 47), unforgivably optimistic lending at several others, and perfectly sensible banking at the rest, which promptly applied to the FDIC and NCUA and quickly reopened.

This book is not intended as a call to arms, or as an investigation into how banking has gone awry, or a history of banking, or even a complete how-to manual. It is a primer on banking language and practice, though many who have heeded a call to arms from some other bugler will find this information useful. Furthermore, this is decidedly *not* a discussion of money, the social consequences of debt, or an introduction to alternatives to our monetary system. Though there are certainly reasons to be dissatisfied with all of that, those topics are well beyond the scope of a small book like this. Nonetheless, this book will equip you to discuss all these topics with confidence and possibly to seem intelligent while doing so, though the details of that masquerade are left to the reader's own efforts, as they always must be.

Banks, banking, and money in general make for a vast and confusing subject. None of the insiders have any incentive to make things clear for onlookers. They use obscure language to describe simple things, and simple language to describe obscure things. I hope to have helped make it a little bit clearer with this book, and its glosssary, and further hope some of you will use the information here to become more effective advocates for changing the way our financial system works, and that some will even help create those new financial institutions our nation so desperately needs.

I would be delighted to hear about omissions I've made or corrections and additions you might think necessary. Contact information is on the copyright page.

Wickford, RI
October, 2013

## One

# Why change the banks?

### The fall of IndyMac

IN NOVEMBER OF 2006, Pasadena's IndyMac Bank, was flying high. Among the nation's largest thrifts,[2] their stock was trading at $75 per share. Riding the wave of the southern California real estate market, and specializing in big loans, they had assets of almost $30 billion, and a string of branches across the lower half of the state. In 2007, they acquired an east coast mortgage company, adding a few billion more in assets, and then it all began to go sour.

IndyMac had specialized in large loans for customers with poor credit. Indeed, IndyMac had been created years before by Countrywide Financial, among the nation's largest mortgage lenders, to do exactly that. Industry procedure for approval of those kinds of loans (called *Alt-A* loans) typically involved a review of the borrower's credit scores, but little else, which is why they were also called *liar loans*. In the fall of 2007, amid a growing wave of foreclosures, investors began to express suspicions about these loans, and IndyMac saw the value of the mortgages in its loan portfolio drop off a cliff. Their stock price dropped too, from $75 to $30 by the end of October.

By the spring of 2008, the stock price had halved again, and the bank barely avoided being forced to give back half a billion in depositors' money by backdating a transfer of money—with the collusion of its bank regulators. By the summer, its stock price was down to 80 cents a share,[3] and on June 27, the bank suffered a

---

[2] A thrift is a savings banks specializing in consumer lending, especially home mortgages.

[3] At this point, New York Senator Chuck Schumer issued a letter of complaint to the regulators, the FDIC and the Office of Thrift Supervision (OTS) saying the

5

classic bank run, complete with thousands of customers crowding its lobbies, just like in the movie, "It's a Wonderful Life," except it was Pasadena in July, so it was more people and hotter than Bedford Falls. Despite frequent public reassurances from the FDIC, customers withdrew $1.3 billion from IndyMac in the course of two weeks. Without enough cash to meet the demands of its customers, IndyMac was shut down by the FDIC. IndyMac cost the FDIC $13 billion, the most costly bank failure to date.

## Philadelphia gambles with its schools

THE PHILADELPHIA SCHOOL DISTRICT is the eighth-largest in the country, with a $2.3 billion operating budget for 242 schools serving 150,000 children, over 80% of whom are poor. The finances of the district, along with the rest of the city, are under a lot of pressure these days. That, of course, makes them no different from a lot of urban school districts. With state aid unable (or unwilling) to keep up with their expenses, and local property taxes pushed up as high as politically possible, the department has been in dire straits for some years.

From 2002 until 2007, the city executed a series of "interest-rate swap" agreements with Wall Street banks, including Wells Fargo, Morgan Stanley, Citigroup and Goldman Sachs, to transform their floating-rate debt into fixed-rate debt. Under these agreements, the Philadelphia school district agreed to pay the dollar value of the fixed-rate debts of the banks, and in exchange those banks agreed to pay the floating-rate debts of the school district. The intent was to make budgeting more predictable, and possibly to save some money. Accounts of what motivated it (and whose idea it was) differ at this point, since things did not turn out well.

Unfortunately for Philadelphia, once the agreements were in place, interest rates plunged in the aftermath of the 2008 financial crisis, and they remain at historic low levels today, five years later. Philadelphia's payments to the banks at the fixed rates didn't plunge, but the payments the banks made to Philadelphia went down to nearly zero. Suddenly, what seemed like a bright idea at the time had become a disaster, and as of 2013, the school district and the city have lost $331 million in these deals, including

---

regulators had let the situation get out of control. Schumer's letter is frequently blamed for the collapse, but the collapse was well underway before then, with the bank's stock having already suffered a 99% loss over the previous 18 months.

interest rate payments and more than $110 million in cancellation fees. They remain on the hook for hundreds of millions more, and the banks have been utterly unwilling to forgive or renegotiate these deals. As of July 2013, the district has plans to close dozens of schools and lay off thousands of employees to deal with their ongoing fiscal crisis.

## The disintegration of Lehman Brothers

WHILE THE IMPLOSION of IndyMac was obviously a sign that the fiscal crisis was deepening, the collapse of Lehman Brothers, the Wall Street investment bank, is regarded as a watershed in the 2008 crisis. Lehman, a bank once worth $600 billion, went bankrupt in September of that year, and it remains the largest bankruptcy filing in US history.

Lehman Brothers was heavily invested in the subprime mortgage market, and owned its own mortgage broker until 2007, when they closed it. The bank was being run with very little margin for error. At the end of 2007, they had borrowed over thirty dollars for every dollar of capital. At this kind of leverage, a loss of just one-thirtieth of the value of their assets would make them insolvent, owing more than they could repay. Lehman was also a heavy user of perfectly legal accounting tricks that allowed them to control investments without having to account for them on their financial reports. If you count the the apparently vast amount of loans they controlled this way—outside of their balance sheet— even smaller losses than that would crash the whole bank.

Unfortunately for a bank relying on such a thin safety margin, Lehman Brothers' assets included a very large quantity of the riskiest mortgage-backed bonds they sold. It's one thing to walk on a tightrope; it's an entirely different thing when the rope is badly frayed. And it's windy. When the market for those bonds began to go south, it didn't take long before Lehman lost all its own money and began to lose money they had borrowed from others. Compounding the crisis, because so many of their assets and liabilities were not on their balance sheet, it became impossible for the banking regulators to find someone to assume Lehman's business. Feeling they had to make an example of Lehman's reckless behavior, Fed chair Ben Bernanke and Treasury Secretary Henry Paulson decided to let Lehman fold, and let the chips fall. And fall they did.

## What does it mean?

Three disasters for taxpayers and other bystanders, three different causes. If you are like a lot of people, these stories are a little hard to follow. Explaining the terms and the components of the processes and deals that make up these stories is the goal of this book. You need the tools to understand what bankers are talking about when they talk about banking.

The examples here were chosen to illustrate some points important to understanding how banks work:

- It's all pretty complicated. If you don't know how banks work, the actions of the various players seem bizarre and even opaque. Certainly greed is behind a lot of bank activity, but it's not the only thing.

- There are different kinds of risk in banking: liquidity risk took down IndyMac, interest rate risk bit the city of Philadelphia, and credit risk sank Lehman Brothers.

- Banks with a lot of leverage are vulnerable to market fluctuations, and the greater the leverage, the less of a drop in value it takes to unleash a catastrophe, and the higher the risk.

- Banks frequently "manage" the risk of banking simply by looking for someone else to take that risk for them, like they did with Philadelphia, or the buyers of IndyMac's and Lehman's mortgage securities. This isn't managing risk at all, but simply shuffling it onto someone less informed about the subject.

The goal of this book is to explain the details of banking so that you can make sense of the causes and effects within each of these examples, to understand the pitfalls of banking as well as the exact location of the magic beans that create much of our economy's money supply. The idea is to try to answer questions like these: *Why* did IndyMac (along with all the other big mortgage originators) think it important to shovel mortgages out the door despite the declining quality of available borrowers? *Why* did Goldman and Citigroup think it important to engage in currency-rate swaps? *Why* did Lehman Brothers continue to think it wise to create so much leverage,[4] and how were they able to hide the off-books stuff?

Banks are a mainstay of our economy. Few manufacturers could run without a line of credit for buying parts and materials. Few people could afford to buy a home without access to credit, and few governments could operate without credit with which to amortize costs over several years. Nor could any of these operate without a safe place to store money. Banks are essential, and yet they often go very wrong, precisely what makes understanding them so important.

Banks' function encompasses not just technical-mechanical issues, but also social ones. The three examples above also tell us other useful information, not limited to the following.

- Despite what you might think, with few and notable exceptions, banks have no "fiduciary duty" (responsibility) to serve their customers. Not in a legal sense, nor in a practical sense. They're supposed to give you back your money when you ask for it, but that's about it.

- The form or size of the bank isn't particularly important. IndyMac was a thrift, a kind of bank meant to do small-scale local consumer lending: single-family mortgages, car loans, and so on. But in reality, IndyMac was taking deposits from southern California, their community, and using them to buy jumbo mortgages from Countrywide, who was arranging loans, well, countrywide.

- Lots of bankers aren't particularly good at their trade. It's astonishing to look at the historical accounts of 2004–2008 and realize that many of the bankers in charge thought their bank's activity was sustainable. Banking is complicated, and it's a fallacy to assume that all bankers understand it equally well.

There's a lot to fix as well as a lot to understand about the incentives that face banks and bankers. Discussion of fixing incentives cannot, of course, excuse the astounding lack of social responsibility exhibited by the CEOs of the nation's largest banks. Bankers at Goldman Sachs and Wells Fargo would rather see

---

[4]Yes, I know, but I mean *besides* the bonuses.

Philadelphia schoolchildren denied music education and guidance counselors than re-assume some of the risk (and resulting losses) they persuaded Philadelphia to take. Bankers at IndyMac felt their bonuses were more important than the potential devastation the wave of foreclosures caused in neighborhoods where they were heavily invested. Bankers at Lehman Brothers were heedless of the risks they were creating for the world financial system, including institutional investors, like pension funds. Sadly, one can go on. These were (and are) appalling lapses, but in many ways, these bankers were responding to incentives external to their banks.

The banking industry lobbied intensively for changes in banking law that produced most of these incentives, so we could just blame it all on greed and be done. Nonetheless, you learn more by studying the incentives and the actors separately than by condemning them all together. The appalling part is how enthusiastically, blindly, and greedily many bankers responded to the incentives, but that's a different matter than understanding the incentives themselves. To do that, you need to understand banking, and how it has evolved over time, first.

## Climate change

Some important and even popular reforms of the last 30 years—such as the democratization of the bond market, the deregulation of interest rates, or the approval of interstate banking—created financial motivations to do what banks have done, both by increasing the rewards, but also by increasing the risks of banking. Other changes, such as the astonishing growth and consolidation of banks, the proliferation of derivative investments, and the devil-may-care culture that encouraged foisting off risk onto unsuspecting clients, were internally generated.

An example will help. In 1980, Congress deregulated the interest rates banks could pay their customers. This was a relatively popular reform,[5] and banks responded by raising the rates they paid, and advertising them. But what also happened was that customer money began to flow *from* the smaller banks who were invested in less-profitable consumer lending *to* the larger ones who

---

[5]I, at least, was delighted at the time, and can't honestly say I understood the consequences until 1991, when the nation was waist-deep in failed S&Ls and Rhode Island, my home state, was suffering its own banking crisis.

could earn more with bigger deals and had alternate sources of income. The small banks were getting squeezed and had to raise the rates they paid to avoid losing their depositors. That, in turn, meant they had to make their lending more profitable. IndyMac found an answer to this puzzle, but not a very good one. The S&L crisis of the late 1980s was largely brought about by bankers at small banks seeking more profitable opportunities and finding more risk along with them. Presumably cupidity drove some of them, but the fact is that the changing regulatory climate had eliminated the stable savings-bank business they had known, so some response was essential.

The growth of banks, made possible by Congressional repeal of rules against interstate banks, has had consequences, too. Banks originally came to exist because of a need to aggregate savings for the purpose of investing. Through the course of history, similar structures developed in several different societies, leading one to the suspicion that there is something fundamentally necessary about banking, at least once you invent money (or debt). But the banks of our history were relatively smaller affairs than the ones dominating the scene today. There was a place for bankers to get to know their customers personally, to be able to assess and manage the risk of banking via their respective ties to the community. In the modern jargon, one calls this *relationship banking*, usually contrasted with the more anonymous *price banking* where price-sensitive customers flow from one bank to another, and decisions about risks are made on the basis of experience with customers and statistical models to identify which customers are relevant to which experiences. One can picture the terms being invented to grace a slide presentation by some banking executive, meant to assure the audience that it was no problem that the bank was to grow far beyond the possibility of maintaining personal relationships with its customers.

## Risky business

The growth of banks from small institutions to large has had profound effects on all of us, not least because of the necessary change in strategies to manage banking risk. When a bank makes a loan, it takes a risk that the loan may not be repaid. Banking is fundamentally about managing that risk, and other risks associated with the enterprise. But there are many ways to manage a risk.

One way is to get to know your borrowers, to assess their needs, perhaps even to help them repay the loan with the occasional extension or refinance. In the case of a business loan, a bank could sometimes ease the risk through introducing the borrower to potential customers for his or her business. Another way to manage risk is simply to find someone else to assume it. One way manages risk by reducing it; the other simply foists it onto a sucker.

Done on a grand scale, these different strategies can have radically different effects on an economy. As banks grow and relationships with customers become more anonymous, relationship banking is necessarily supplanted by price banking. Managing risk through relationships must give way to managing risk by finding suckers, with all that this entails.

In these and many other ways, the climate of the banking market has changed dramatically since a generation ago. The important thing about changing climate is that it changes ecological niches in fundamental ways. Some ways of living cease to be possible. Organisms that cannot adapt to the new climate, die—which is why we live in a world dominated by mammals instead of dinosaurs. The banks and financial institutions that dominate our world a generation from now may look nothing like the ones that do today, for better or worse. At some small risk of cornballery, it's worthwhile to point out that we have a democracy, more or less, so therefore the job of ensuring that the coming changes are for the better falls to each of us.

As you read this book, please do so while asking the question, how can you use the information here to help build those better financial institutions.

- Can you figure out a way to start a credit union, that perhaps improves on the models widely used today?

- Can you imagine a bank that does a better job of supporting its community and the kinds of economic activity you want to encourage?

- If you are an official of a city, town, county, or state, can you see a way to stop being a mere customer of Wall Street, and create financial institutions to wield the financial clout your government's assets should merit?

None of these questions will be easy to answer, but the future belongs to the people who figure out the right solutions.

## Reading this book

We begin with the basics. Chapter 2 of *Checking the Banks* covers the basics of banking, including balance sheet accounting and the regulatory ratios that bank regulators use to analyze a bank's condition. You'll find a discussion there of bank capital and why it's so confusing, sample balance sheets of actual banks, and a look at the kinds of measurements bank regulators use to assess a bank's health.

Chapter 3 discusses the actual operation of a bank, including the kinds of risks a bank's management must navigate, and the tools at their disposal, the other players in the field, and the financial terrain. It also describes where bankers hide the magic beans with which they grow money.

Chapter 4 looks a little more deeply at some important regulatory issues and developments, including the questions of how banks and regulators evaluate risk and what they do about it. All of these chapters are meant only as introductions to the subjects. Any of the subsections are worth a book of their own.

The second half of this book is addressed not just to the student of banks, but to the activist who might attempt to establish something new. Chapter 5 discusses the mechanics of starting a bank, from the conceptual level, along with some of the basics of preparing a believable business plan. This material is only meant as a supplement to what is available from the bank regulators themselves. The FDIC and OCC web sites contain a wealth of information on the subject, too, including sample business plans, FAQ lists, and sample financial reports from startup banks. There are thousands of ways to go about starting a financial institution, but one hard and fast rule is that no one should contemplate an endeavour like this without spending quality time browsing those web sites.

Chapter 6 is a brief look at the ways in which local, county, and state governments are customers of banks. A great deal of Americans' collective wealth is held by these governments; these are assets that could be harnessed to reshape the banking market.

Finally, Chapter 7 presents some possibilities for new institutions. None of these will be usable as presented, due to differing state laws and local economic and fiscal conditions. They are presented here as a stimulus to the imagination of those who read that far.

## Two

# Bank accounting made simple(r)

BANKS EXIST in what may seem a topsy-turvy world of accounting, where money they are given counts as a liability, and money they lend counts as an asset. Banks even have their own generally accepted accounting principles, different from normal companies.[6] Accounting is a legendarily complicated field, but at root it's pretty simple. Accounting is just a set of rules to follow and things to measure that will help you answer the questions you're likely to need answered. For a bank, the most important questions are, "Are we making money?" and "At what level of risk?" Bank accounting is just a collection of rules and measurements that make it easy to answer those questions.

## Bank accounting 101

The first order of business is to explain why bank accounting seems odd. The answer is simply that it makes the *accounting equation* (Assets = Liabilities + Capital) work out neatly. This relationship is typically laid out in a *balance sheet*, a ledger divided into two sides. The assets are added up on one side and the liabilities and capital added up on the other. When the two sides match—they balance—that's how the accountants know they've done it right. (See figure 2.1.) The important thing here is that this

---

[6]The GAAP are promulgated by the Financial Accounting Standards Board (FASB), a bunch of accountants in Connecticut who define for everyone what good accounting means. Insurance companies and governments have their own principles, too, but that's pretty much all the exceptions.

15

equation is a definition, not an observation or a measurement or a hypothesis. It *must* be true for any business that the stuff it has is equal to the stuff it owns plus the stuff it has and owes to someone else. Accountants use the accounting equation as a check to make sure they've done everything correctly. If you have books that don't balance, you haven't made a discovery, you're doing it wrong.[7]

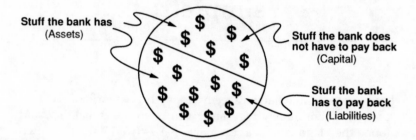

Figure 2.1: *Accounting equation: Assets = Liabilities + Capital. It's not just a good idea, it's a definition. Stuff the bank has (assets) is always equal to the stuff it owes someone (liabilities) plus the stuff it owns and doesn't owe to anyone (capital). This is the foundation of double-entry bookkeeping, and applies to all kinds of assets, from money to buildings to furniture. Anyone who tells you otherwise is probably trying to sell you something you shouldn't buy.*

## Assets

A corporation's *assets* are, generally speaking, the objects and entities it uses to make money. Banks are—or should be—in the business of loaning money in order to earn money, so their loans count as their assets. This does seem odd, since loans are money that's gone out the door, but a loan is money that goes out the door with a promise to be returned along with the interest on that money.

A bank's outstanding loans are not its only assets. Likely it owns some cash, too, and possibly some intellectual property, desks and chairs, real estate, and maybe the office carpets and a

---

[7] If you doubt the accountants, you can rely instead on Aristotle, whose logical rule of the excluded middle says that money a bank possesses (assets) must be made up of money it owns (capital) plus money it does not own (liabilities), and there is no third alternative. It also says the money must be either green or not green, the President's name is either Obama or it is not, etc.

couple of private jets for the CEO. These are all assets, and they all appear on the bank's balance sheet.

## Liabilities

When you deposit money in a bank, in a legal sense the bank is not simply keeping the money for you. They are actually taking your money in exchange for a *liability* to you, just the same way you do when you borrow money from a friend. The bank owes you that money, plus whatever interest it has promised. Since the deposit represents money it owes to you, it counts among the bank's liabilities.

Bankers will often refer to the *cost of funds*, the overhead required to acquire and manage some class of deposits. The cost of funds is usually expressed as an interest rate, for easy comparison to the interest rates the bank charges on its loans. For example, if a bank has calculated that its cost of funds is 0.5%, then it can make money with those funds by lending at 0.6%.[8]

Just as its assets are more than its loans, a bank's liabilities are more varied than just its deposits, and will include accrued rent to its landlords, salaries to its employees, the cost of unpaid sexual harassment judgments, and so on. Like the assets, all of these liabilities will (or should) appear on a bank's balance sheet.

## Capital

Bank *capital* is widely misunderstood, but it's not your fault. Bankers and regulators use the word in an irritatingly wide variety of contexts. The basic definition is simple: a bank's capital is money it doesn't have to pay back to anyone. It's also called a bank's *equity*, which may be a less confusing term to use. Generally speaking, the equity was originally put up by the investors who will own the bank.

There are a couple of different forms a bank's starting capital can take. A commercial bank might sell stock, while for a mutual bank or a credit union certain kinds of restricted deposits count as capital. But put the variations aside for a moment: for any variant

---

[8]A margin that small won't work once you include reserve requirements and lots of other details to come, but it's still useful shorthand.

of a bank (or any company, for that matter) capital is just the stuff the bank doesn't have to pay back. The *owners* of a bank might have to repay money they borrowed in order to found a bank, but that's different from the bank itself having to pay it back.

The other important component of capital is *retained profit* or *retained earnings*. Money the bank does not pay in dividends to its owners is kept by the bank, and while the owners might have some kind of claim on that money, it's no different than the claim they have on the rest of the company. A bank's ownership structure can be complicated, so the question of how much capital there is can be complicated to answer, but the bottom line[9] is the same: it's stuff the bank doesn't have to pay back to anyone. You'll see this on reports sometimes as *bank equity capital* and books will sometimes call it *accounting capital*.

## Reserves

Here's what capital *isn't*: money kept on hand to pay a bank's day-to-day liabilities. That money—made up of actual cash, along with reserve accounts at the Federal *Reserve* bank, or with banks that have accounts at the Fed—is called a bank's *reserves*, or should be. Unfortunately, when a bank's reserves are too low, we often say the bank is "undercapitalized" or bring up the capital requirements or the Basel Accords. In an accounting sense, you could say this is loose talk, and it's more accurate to talk about reserves and reserve requirements. The loose talk is bad for clarity, but good for preserving the mystique of banking, because it leaves everyone else confused. After all, the whole purpose behind jargon is to have a way to tell the insiders from the outsiders.

Part of the source of the confusion is the accounting. Reserves are an asset of a bank, while capital is on the other side of the balance sheet. Balance sheets have to balance, so if the assets go up, either the capital or liabilities or both have to increase to maintain the balance. A bank can deal with a chronic reserve shortage by selling shares in the (wait for it)...capital markets. But reserve shortfalls are also typically addressed by: borrowing in the Fed funds market; secured borrowing through repurchase transactions with other banks (see footnote on page 64); lying about the

---

[9]Accounting slang. Isn't this fun?

value of bank assets; making a profit; or all of the above.[10] Each of these will increase the reserves (an asset) and affect the balance sheet somewhere else, to keep it balanced. Increasing profit will increase the capital, while borrowing reserve funds from other banks will increase the liabilities.

*In the next section, we'll work through some example balance sheets. You may find it easier to follow the examples with a pad and pencil handy. Make yourself a balance sheet by dividing a piece of paper in half and putting assets on one side and capital and liabilities on the other side. When the two sides add up to the same amount— they balance—you've done it right.*

## Balance sheets

Imagine for a moment a bank that has $1 billion in loans out there. We'll call it the Bank of Sunnydale. They're charging an average of 3% interest, so there's about $30 million in income each year. Suppose expenses take half of that, leaving $15 million for the shareholders. Suppose further that this bank has $100 million in capital, from its shareholders. Each investor is therefore getting approximately a 15% return (15 divided by 100) on his or her investment, which isn't terrible.

In the USA, the *reserve requirement* is 10% for *demand deposits* like checking accounts (sometimes called *transaction accounts*), and zero for *time deposits*, accounts with a fixed term, like CDs. Of course it's more complicated than this, with smaller requirements for smaller institutions, and exemptions for the first $25 million under these conditions, and so on, but that's the rough rule. If bank management, given their mix of customer accounts, thinks they need 5% of their total deposit base in cash to meet their

---

[10]Or by getting the Fed to loan it money at 0.25% and using that to buy Treasury bonds at 2%. This is what the Fed did after the financial meltdown of 2008, to, um, recapitalize the remaining big banks.

An alternative was presented by the Office of Thrift Supervision (OTS), a federal bank regulator, that assisted several banks in backdating their acquisition of capital. As we saw in Chapter 1, IndyMac did this in 2008, and the West Division director resigned when his complicity in hiding the transaction came to light. In 2009, the OTS director resigned after acknowledging four similar cases. In other words, another strategy for covering a reserve shortfall is to try to get the regulator to cover it up. Sadly, OTS has been dissolved so bankers of tomorrow will have to suborn a different regulatory agency in order to use this strategy.

liquidity needs, then the bank's balance sheet will look (very roughly) like this:

| Assets | Liabilities & Capital |
|---|---|
| $1 billion loans | $950 million deposits |
| $50 million cash | $100 million capital |
| $1.05 billion | $1.05 billion |

The 5% reserve of $950 million is about $50 million, and that's what the bank has in cash and cash equivalents: bags of actual coins and bills, along with accounts at the *Federal Reserve Bank*, usually called the *Fed*, or at other banks who have accounts there if Sunnydale does not have one. The Fed is the central bank of the United States, and gets its name from being the place where banks hold their reserves. Remember this about reserves: cash pays no interest, and the accounts at the Fed only started paying interest after the financial crisis of 2008, but it is not much. (How long they will continue to do so is an open question.) This is effectively money the bank can't invest in anything, and any bank will seek to minimize this, on efficiency grounds alone.

Now suppose the bank examiner comes along and says the bank has not calculated its proportion of accounts correctly, or reclassifies their extra-special renewable CDs as transaction accounts, and they therefore don't have enough...capital.[11] What they mean with their loose talk is that the bank doesn't have adequate reserves to defend against the *liquidity risk* it has undertaken (see page 46), or they have other reasons to be skeptical about the level of reserves. The regulators are worried that more people than Sunnydale has anticipated might want their money back and the bank won't have it to pay out. Whatever it is, they want Sunnydale to increase its capital—to increase the amount of money the bank doesn't owe to anyone—*in order to beef up its reserves*.

Increasing reserves is unpopular among the bank shareholders because it dilutes the value of each share. Suppose the regulator demands the bank get its reserves up to $70 million ASAP. The difference between that and what they already have is more than a whole year's net revenue, so the bank turns to the capital markets,

---

[11]This is a cartoon version of what the examiners would say, but go with it for the moment because it's a cartoon bank. Regulators would have more to complain about Sunnydale's managers than this, but leave that for later.

and sells $20 million in shares. Now all's good, and the balance sheet looks like this:

| Assets | Liabilities & Capital |
|---|---|
| $1 billion loans | $950 million deposits |
| $70 million cash | $120 million capital |
| $1.07 billion | $1.07 billion |

The only problem is that now the shareholders are only earning 12.5% on their investment (15/120), and they're unhappier than they were before. Boo hoo, but this is why banks resist increasing capital requirements: the shareholders' return on investment goes down.[12]

This is one way "capital" and "reserves" get confused. The bank raised capital (one side of the balance sheet) in order to increase its reserves (an asset on the other side), but they are very different things. This is an appallingly simplified example, and the bank could have increased its reserves by borrowing, which would have increased the liabilities instead, or other ways.[13] This example was chosen to illustrate how the two terms can easily be confused.

## A closer look at balance sheets

But wait, you might say. Doesn't the Bank of Sunnydale own its headquarters building? If the balance sheet contains everything the bank owns, where is that?

The Bank of Sunnydale's imaginary balance sheet on page 19 is highly simplified in order to explain important points and introduce the idea of regulatory ratios. In reality, part of what the

---

[12]Of course the investors' risk goes down, too, but it seems nobody ever wants to hear about that *before* the disaster.

[13]For example, a bank in trouble could try some creative accounting to prevent anyone from noticing the problem in the first place. In 2011, BankAmerica reported $6.2 billion in net income for the third quarter, $4.5 billion of which of which was due to changes in valuation of its assets. Billions of dollars of those assets were the toxic mortgage bonds that sank AIG, and the market for them had disappeared. But Fed-approved accounting changes enacted in the aftermath of the 2008 meltdown allowed BofA to keep them on their books at the value BofA thought they ought to be instead of using the value they could actually get for them. An inflated value for their assets would be balanced by an (apparent) increase in the value of the capital.

investors originally put up would be spent to establish the bank operation: to buy the building, the software to run the loan operation, the furniture for employees to sit on, or the artwork for customers to admire while they wait. The original stake is usually also used to pay the legal costs of founding the bank, and sometimes even for employee salaries. Out of that original stake used to found Sunnydale, it will surprise no one if a lot of it is spent and isn't ever coming back as loanable cash.[14]

We've been looking at the Sunnydale bank as if it has been running for a while. Let's add some detail as we look for a moment at the process of starting it up at the very beginning.

## A bank is born

ONCE UPON A TIME, a bunch of Sunnydale movers and shakers got together and decided to start a bank. They announced they would sell a million shares at $30 apiece to raise the capital. Because everyone thinks so highly of these movers and shakers, they sell their $30 million of shares for $50 million, O happy day. On day one, this is all the money they have, and their balance sheet might look like this:

| Assets | Liabilities & Capital |
|---|---|
| $0 loans | $0 deposits |
| $10 million building, artwork | |
| $5 million intangibles | |
| $30 million securities | $30 million stock |
| $5 million cash | $20 million surplus |
| $50 million | $50 million |

The "cash" line of the assets will be both cash and deposits at other banks (possibly including the Fed if Sunnydale becomes a member). You can think of the "intangibles" line in the balance sheet as representing things like business relationships and intellectual property, or you can think of it as money spent on legal fees

[14]It's also worth noting here that though we're spending a great deal of attention on balance sheets, a bank's *income statement* (also its *profit-and-loss*, or *P&L*, statement) is also an important part of analyzing a bank's operation. The income statement identifies the sources of a bank's income (and losses), and can be quite revealing when you're looking into a bank's operation. Regulators can be just as interested in a bank's income statement as in its balance sheet.

and other costs of getting the bank underway. Either way is correct; it's a record of how much was spent on expenses that didn't produce something with a market value. The "surplus" line is the difference between the face value of the shares ($30 million) and the price they got for them ($20 million). The face value is how the founders divide up voting rights among the shareholders, so it's important to keep track of that number and not mix it up with the actual price. Bottom line (not a figure of speech): total assets, $50 million, total liabilities, zero, total capital, $50 million. The accounting equation is satisfied.[15]

Starting on day one, and assuming those movers and shakers continue to move and shake, people will bring in deposits and take out loans, and the balance sheet will grow. But that $5 million invested in the intangibles isn't ever coming back in liquid form, and the $10 million on the buildings, furniture, and artwork probably won't come back intact, either. Because accountants and regulators tend to be sticklers, they'll continue to insist that this money appear on the balance sheet in some form, but it is not going to be spent on anything else, or loaned out.

After a little while, the balance sheet might look like this:

| Assets | Liabilities & Capital |
|---|---|
| $30 million loans | $9 million deposits |
| ($3 million) loan loss allowance | |
| $10 million building, artwork | |
| $5 million intangibles | $1 million retained profit |
| $10 million securities | $30 million stock |
| $5 million cash | $17 million surplus |
| $57 million | $57 million |

The bank has loaned out $30 million of its original stake, and so far has earned a million in profit which it has added to its capital. (This is a high rate of return, but then again, this is an imaginary bank.) The $30 million in loans appears in the balance sheet with a negative $3 million loan loss allowance, because we're assuming that 10% of the loans will go bad.[16] The surplus has been

---

[15]The accounting equation, of course, is *always* satisfied, which is what it means to be a definition. We just use it as a check that we're doing the accounting right.

[16]It is nothing but a convention among bankers that this is booked as a negative number on the asset side of the balance sheet instead of being booked as a liability. Think of it as the accounting version of driving on the right side of the road.

adjusted down accordingly to match. Sunnydale has also taken in $9 million in deposits. Total assets, $57 million, total liabilities, $9 million, total capital, $48 million.

So how strong a bank is Sunnydale? They have plenty of reserves with which to manage their depositors. But liquidity risk isn't the only risk banks face. Shockingly, sometimes loans are not repaid. This is called *credit risk*. Sunnydale has accounted for this by keeping a loan loss allowance on their books, but that's not all they do. They also try to keep enough money around so that a loan going bad or some other unforeseen event won't wreak some other kind of havoc. What if a flood knocks out one of their branches, or they lose a suit over racial preferences in their lending? What if the interest rates they have to pay depositors rises above the 3% they're getting on their loans? The reserves protect liquidity, but something else has to protect the reserves. Remember, the reserves are as much insurance as they are just money you need to have around to manage the cash demands of your customers. Without that insurance, managers could quickly be eating into their cash reserve if something unexpected happens, increasing the risk of a liquidity crisis.

Bank regulators, it turns out, don't just care about reserve ratios, but also about the total amount of money the bank has (or could have) on hand, compared to the total amount of the risks it has (or could have) taken on. Think of it this way: a $10 bet in a poker game means a lot more to someone who only has $20 in chips remaining than it does to someone who holds $1000. Another way that "capital" is used is to refer to *financial capital*, or what you might think of as the pile of poker chips the bank owns.[17] This measure of a bank's health is the *capital adequacy ratio*, or *CAR*, and is defined by dividing the pile-of-chips version of capital with the risk-of-the-bets version of the bank's assets. Numbers more than 10% are considered sound. For Sunnydale, this would be $48 million (total capital) divided by $27 million (value of invested assets), or 177%, so they're fine. Of course they're just starting out, so they haven't had a chance to build up much of a loan portfolio, another way to say they haven't had time to do anything wrong.

---

[17]The attentive reader will point out that for most banks the size of the bets is usually way bigger than the pile of chips, because so many of the bets are made with borrowed money. To tell the truth, those attentive readers are kind of a pain, but it is true that the poker analogy can only go just so far.

In Sunnydale's case, were they to lose all the loans they'd made at this stage, they would doubtless be depressed and demoralized, but none of their depositors would be at risk of losing any money. They'd still have $15 million in cash and securities to repay $9 million in deposits, so have plenty of room before anyone had to consider selling the headquarters or the CEO's limo.

You'll frequently hear people talk about *Tier 1 capital* or *Tier 2 capital*. The names stem from the Basel Accords, the series of international banking agreements that were supposed to create more security for the international financial system.[18] As is typical in agreements like these, the distinctions are fine and complicated. After all, the banks spend a lot of time lobbying government officials to make these regulations favorable to themselves, and that gets reflected in very complicated definitions. But as is also typical, the intent of the regulations is straightforward, however byzantine the elaborations and compromises made en route to an actual agreement.

The short version is that Tier 1 capital is supposed to be capital that measures the strength of the bank—the bank could lose it and if not still operate, at least not lose customer deposits—while Tier 2 is useful capital, but maybe shouldn't be counted as contributing to a bank's strength, possibly because some of it is already dedicated to anticipated losses, like a loan loss allowance allocation. Roughly speaking, Tier 1 capital is the value of the stock plus retained earnings, minus intangible assets. For Sunnydale, the Tier 1 capital would be the accountants' definition of equity *minus* the intangibles: $48 million, minus $5 million, or $43 million. The Tier 2 capital would be the loan loss allowance, or $3 million. Sunnydale possesses this money, but has already allocated it to expected losses in its loan portfolio.

## Capital reality check

You can see here how the accounting definition of capital and the bank regulation version have parted company in some sense. The accountants want to count the intangible stuff because it explains where the money went, while the bank regulators don't want to

---

[18]Ha, ha, but that's another story. The short version is just that these agreements, initiated in 1988, began with the best of noble intentions, but have too often become ways for international banks to undercut regulation by national banking authorities.

count it because it doesn't contribute to the financial strength of the bank. Alternatively, the Tier 1 capital includes the value of tangible-but-not-liquid assets, like the bank headquarters. In theory a bank could afford to lose such an asset and stay in business, but reality is crueler. Such a bank would quickly suffer a run by its depositors and be closed by the FDIC or be forced to sell its performing assets to a competitor for pennies on the dollar.

Reviewing a bunch of bank balance sheets, one sees that they tend to have more or less the value of their capital around in relatively liquid form. Theoretically, this is not necessary, but since a bank ought to be prepared to lose its capital it makes a certain amount of sense. A loan that goes bad is just a balance sheet adjustment, but some risks involve real potential losses, and protecting depositors' funds is almost a synonym for protecting the owners from being liable for losses. How a bank addresses all these issues is an important part of its business strategy.

Here is a somewhat more realistic balance sheet for Sunnydale than the one on page 19, after a few years of operation. They've grown by taking in more deposits and lending out more money, adding to the retained profit component of their capital. The stock and surplus remain the same as before, presumably because the retained profit has grown enough that it can be used to balance the loan loss allowance.[19] It's still a billion-dollar operation, but the asset allocation is a little more in line with what is usually done.

| Assets | Liabilities & Capital |
|---|---|
| $880 million loans | $950 million deposits |
| ($80 million) loan loss allowance | |
| $10 million building, artwork | |
| $5 million intangibles | $53 million retained profit |
| $185 million securities | $30 million stock |
| $50 million cash | $17 million surplus |
| $1.05 billion | $1.05 billion |

The assets are now spread into other categories, but the big difference is that the Sunnydale managers are keeping a fair amount

---

[19]In an accounting sense, Sunnydale could compensate by reducing the value of the stock, too, but companies don't like to admit their stock value has declined, so when there are alternatives, they almost always take them. After all, the people making management decisions probably own a lot of stock themselves.

of the bank's assets as securities instead of as loans. They haven't loaned out everything. The shareholders are earning a little bit less than they did before, since the securities do not pay as high a rate as the loan portfolio.[20] On the brighter side, it's a much less risky operation overall, with ample reserves, but also a padding of securities to protect the reserves. Plus the securities can be used as collateral for borrowing at the Fed discount window or for borrowing in the "repo" market (see page 64). There is less risk on their balance sheet, but there's still plenty of leverage. The CAR stands at about 10%, which is within the bounds of sanity.

## Accounting for risk

So now we have a definition of capital that is different than the accounting definition, but more useful for measuring the strength of the bank. Divide by the assets and we have a good measure of risk, right?

Not so fast.

Some of a bank's assets are riskier than others, even if they appear to have the same value. For example, collection of T-bills worth $1 million might have the same face value as a collection of mortgage-backed bonds worth $1 million, but there is a lot less risk in the T-bills. So bank regulators devised a way to weight the assets by their risk when you're adding them up. The idea is to count the assets according to the amount you think could go bad. The cash can't go bad, so you don't count that at all. The mortgages could go bad, but usually not as often as the business loans, which are in turn less risky than the investments in credit default swaps. The result is the *risk-weighted assets* or *RWA*. You can think of the RWA as the sum of the asset risk: on the worst possible day the bankers who run the bank imagine having, this is how much it would lose.

---

[20]This, incidentally, was the great appeal behind the mortgage-backed bond mania of 2000–2008. By "tranching" the bonds (see "Subdividing bonds" on page 135), banks could create securities that appeared to have as little risk as Treasury bonds, but paid rates as high as the loan portfolio. They were wrong about the risk, of course. And wrong about the rates, too, for that matter.

Looking at Sunnydale again, a further breakdown of its assets might look like this:

| | | |
|---|---|---|
| Mortgage loans | $400 million × 50% | = $200 million |
| Business loans | $480 million × 80% | = $384 million |
| Mortgage bonds | $100 million × 100% | = $100 million |
| Treasury securities | $85 million × 0% | = $0 |
| Fixed assets | $15 milion × 100% | = $15 million |
| Cash & equivalents | $50 million × 0% | = $0 |
| **Total** | $1.05 billion | |
| **Weighted total** | | = $699 million |

The weights are applied according to the risk of the assets. Cash and US Treasury bills (*T-bills*) are essentially without risk, while a lot of the mortgage loans in circulation now have been shown to be pretty risky. What this is saying is that $699 million of the bank's assets are at risk—these are bets with a real risk of failing—and this is the appropriate number to compare to the amount of financial capital the bank owns. For Sunnydale, the Tier 1 capital is $95 million ($100 million in capital minus $5 million in intangibles), so the risk-weighted CAR (sometimes called the *CRAR*) is $95/$699, or about 13.5%.[21] The FDIC term of art for a bank with a CRAR of more than 10% is "well-capitalized," and Sunnydale meets that standard. At 8-10%, a bank is called "adequately capitalized" and below that is "under-capitalized." If Sunnydale's exchanged some of its assets to be riskier, the ratio will go down. What happens if it allocates more money to mortgage bonds and less to mortgages it underwrites? What happens if it take on more business lending and less mortgage lending? What happens if it invests more capital in a new building?

There's an important distinction here that is all too often blurred. The CAR is a good measure of the riskiness of a bank's

---

[21]The weights used here are just for illustration. They are subject to frequent debate and change in the real world. For example, business loans are (currently) considered to be more risky than mortgage loans because that was the experience in financial crises before 2008. That was not the experience in that crisis, but the widespread use of risk-weighting with that assumption built in meant that business lending plunged in the aftermath. Under Basel III, some of the new weights for the riskiest assets may exceed 100% but it's not clear who verifies that risk or justifies the weights. Consider that the 2008 crisis was triggered because supposedly safe assets (AAA-rated subprime mortgage bonds) turned out to be not safe at all, not because banks were loading up on assets known to be risky.

capital structure while the risk weighting is a measure of the riskiness of the assets in which a bank has invested. The CRAR combines the two, and it's useful shorthand, but it's really mixing up two different concepts—the riskiness of the assets and the riskiness of the capital structure—into the same measurement. A bank with a high CAR (low leverage) but lots of risky assets is in a different situation from a bank with a low CAR invested very safely, though they might have the same CRAR.

For example, think of a bank with capital equal to 50% of its assets (CAR = 50%), but the assets are all loans to poker players about to enter a tournament. Compare that to a highly-leveraged bank with capital only 1% of its assets, but 98% of its assets are government bonds and the other 2% of loans are to those same poker players. These banks will have the same CRAR.

In one sense these banks are in a similar position, since their capital only covers half of some very risky assets, but they will require very different strategies to address the deficiencies. The first one needs to replace a lot of its assets with less risky investments while the second needs more capital. Trying to make either bank take the other's medicine would be silly.[22]

All the variables here, the various kinds of capital, the RWA, and other items on the balance sheet, are used by regulators and CFOs to generate a whole array of ratios and indicators beyond the ones we've discussed.[23] They are all meant to quantify the level of risk a bank has undertaken. You have to get them right in order to come up with a plausible proposal for a bank, but when spitballing ideas, you can usually satisfy them by just using common sense—after you've spent some time thinking about what common sense means to a bank.

There are a lot of gray areas in this work. The FDIC evaluation of a bank's liquidity rests in a set of liquidity management guidelines they publish. Examiners are supposed to evaluate the actual risks and use judgment, so mileage varies pretty dramati-

---

[22]The distinction between the two forms of risk is especially important because the riskiness of a bank's structure can be measured accurately with great precision, while the riskiness of assets cannot be measured precisely *or* accurately. Imprecision is contagious, so combining these two numbers into a single measurement is therefore flouting one of the fundamental rules of data analysis: don't let your bad measurements infect your good ones.

[23]Rather than try to calculate them yourself for a particular bank, they are available in the Uniform Bank Performance Reports you can get from www.ffiec.gov.

cally, and any bank can have a perfectly valid reason for deviating from the norm for some regulatory ratio. Recently, banks have been turning to more complicated ways to keep themselves liquid, relying on selling bonds (borrowing in the bond market), or on off-balance sheet tricks, and so regulating this has become trickier.[24] The most recent round of the Basel Accords contains regulations concerning overall liquidity that are to be implemented in 2015.

# Example balance sheets

It's all well and good to theorize some balance sheets to talk about them, but theory only takes you just so far. Let's look at some real-world balance sheets to understand what's going on. You can find balance sheets for any bank at the FDIC's web site. It's educational to browse the banks you know about.

Table 2.1 on page 31 contains the balance sheets, as reported to the FDIC, of three different banks. One is Washington Trust, a medium-size bank that serves not much more than the state of Rhode Island. The next is Citizens Bank, a fairly large institution and pioneer in interstate banking that is now owned by the Royal Bank of Scotland, and the third is BankAmerica, a behemoth Too-Big-To-Fail bank. Table 2.2 shows the same data for the Bank of North Dakota (BND), the nation's only public bank. Let's run down the components that make up the Assets, Liabilities, and Capital.

Assets first: this is the sum of the stuff the bank actually has. This includes assets with which the bank makes money, like loans and securities, as well as assets that just sit there, like cash, buildings, and carpets.

**Cash and due from other banks** Includes all coins and bills, as well as any deposits at other banks (sometimes called *correspondent banks*). This includes reserve funds held on account at the Federal Reserve.

---

[24]You'll hear sometimes that the Fed funds market works so well that it is the real source of protection against liquidity risk, not those old-fashioned reserves. This is one of those statements that's only vaguely true. A bank can, in fact, borrow to cover a cash shortfall, but it better have a strategy to pay it back. Otherwise it has merely traded liquidity risk for interest rate risk. As of 2014, that might seem like a good trade, but will it always?

| (numbers in thousands) | Wash. Trust | RBS Citizens | BankAmerica |
|---|---|---|---|
| **Total assets** | **3,044,725** | **107,214,881** | **1,658,890,050** |
| Cash and due from other banks | 48,080 | 9,223,473 | 153,430,070 |
| Securities | 487,322 | 10,373,672 | 342,649,185 |
| Fed funds sold & reverse repo | 0 | 0 | 18,635,426 |
| Net loans & leases | 2,261,354 | 72,345,497 | 872,166,483 |
| Loan loss allowance | 30,752 | 1,121,499 | 25,830,910 |
| Trading account assets | 4,115 | 997,997 | 81,879,113 |
| Bank premises and fixed assets | 27,482 | 1,107,902 | 10,519,485 |
| Other real estate owned | 2,447 | 86,812 | 3,561,988 |
| Goodwill and other intangibles | 65,213 | 9,488,329 | 66,047,618 |
| All other assets | 148,712 | 3,591,199 | 110,000,682 |
| **Total liabilities and capital** | **3,044,725** | **107,214,881** | **1,658,890,050** |
| **Total liabilities** | **2,718,371** | **88,455,001** | **1,450,487,508** |
| Total deposits | 2,236,573 | 79,088,025 | 1,229,906,284 |
| Interest-bearing deposits | 1,882,329 | 57,025,176 | 843,209,101 |
| Fed funds purchased & repo | 0 | 2,928,499 | 61,595,984 |
| Trading liabilities | 4,249 | 940,558 | 37,098,930 |
| Other borrowed funds | 417,904 | 4,013,145 | 67,406,635 |
| All other liabilities | 59,645 | 1,484,774 | 38,704,865 |
| **Total bank equity capital** | **326,354** | **18,759,880** | **206,633,774** |
| Stock | 3,000 | 76 | 4,296,843 |
| Surplus | 172,241 | 16,350,198 | 184,115,344 |
| Retained profits | 151,113 | 2,409,606 | 18,221,587 |

*Table 2.1: Balance sheets for the medium-size Washington Trust bank, the large regional RBS Citizens, and the conventional banking parts of the huge national BankAmerica. You can see that Washington Trust, a community-oriented bank is likely almost loaned out, with only a couple of percent of its total deposits in cash (these are the reserves), whereas Citizens and BankAmerica have over 10%. This probably reflects both regulators' demands that these big banks rebuild their reserves (notice BofA's large loan loss allowance), and the slack in borrowing demand in the economy. You can also see that both BofA and Citizens borrow substantially in the Fed funds and repo markets, while only BofA lends in them. (source: fdic.gov, 9/30/2012 data)*

**Bank of North Dakota**

*(numbers in thousands)*

| | |
|---|---:|
| **Total assets** | **5,868,996** |
| Cash and due from other banks | 500,778 |
| Securities | 2,125,236 |
| Federal funds sold & reverse repo agreements | 39,350 |
| Net loans & leases | 3,136,109 |
| Loan loss allowance | 54,259 |
| Other assets | 67,523 |
| **Total liabilities and capital** | **5,868,996** |
| **Total liabilities** | **5,428,411** |
| Total deposits | 4,842,545 |
| Interest-bearing deposits | 4,240,752 |
| Federal funds purchased & repo agreements | 172,200 |
| Other borrowed funds | 407,011 |
| All other liabilities | 6,655 |
| **Total Bank Equity Capital** | **440,585** |
| Stock | 2,000 |
| Surplus | 42,000 |
| Retained profits | 396,585 |

*Table 2.2: Balance sheet for* Bank of North Dakota *(BND), the only public bank in the country (for now). As in table 2.1, the total amount of loans outstanding is the sum of the "net loans" and the loan loss allowance. The $2 million in common stock is the 1919 founding capital of the bank. Because the bank is owned by the state, it will never sell more stock, so the $2 million will never change. Think of it as an accounting fossil. (source: banknd.nd.gov, 9/31/2012 quarterly report)*

**Securities** Some securities, such as US Government bonds, are just nearly-liquid stores of money. Other securities are purchased when the bank can't find enough loans to fill out its portfolio. You can see that BofA relies on securities far more than the smaller two banks. This heading contains both low-risk, highly-liquid bonds as well as much higher-risk investments, so this category can be misleading.

**Federal funds sold & reverse repo agreements** This is money the bank has loaned to other banks. *Fed funds* loans are typically unsecured, and have very short terms, like one day, and are usually made to satisfy somebody's liquidity needs. A *repurchase agreement* (also *repo*) is also a short-term loan, generally for the same purposes, but are secured by some collateral— the stuff to be repurchased.

**Net loans & leases**  This is the dollar amount of all the loans outstanding *minus* the loan loss allowance. It is normal to account for the bank's credit risk right on the asset side of the balance sheet like this. This is a more realistic assessment of the value of the outstanding loans than simply relying on their face value so it makes some sense to account for it this way instead of with a compensating liability.

**Loan loss allowance**  The bank assumes that this amount of the outstanding loans won't be repaid—it's the dollar value of the bank's credit risk exposure. A bank can appear more profitable by reducing this number, so it's best to read this value as the estimate of the credit risk that has survived pressure from upper management to report higher profits. You'll often see this as a *loan loss reserve*.

**Trading account assets**  This definition is tricky, but in essence, these are assets traded for the bank's own benefit, as opposed to its customers. Because it's theoretically not customer money at risk, the regulations about what kinds of investments are proper are less stringent, and banks can invest in derivatives and short selling and other unspeakable acts. Unfortunately, because these all happen within the same bank, the distinction is usually nearly meaningless in a practical sense. When Nick Leeson and his unauthorized-but-encouraged trading destroyed Barings Bank in 1995, it was with bets made on that bank's trading account.[25] The "Volcker Rule" was a proposal to prevent banks from most of this kind of trading. Endorsed by the Obama administration in 2010, much of it made it into the Dodd-Frank bill, though substantially watered down. Quite a lot more water has been added since the passage of the bill, in the drafting of the regulations to "enforce" it.

---

[25] As of 2013, there was an entertaining article under "rogue traders" at Wikipedia that shows how far from unusual this kind of loss is. The article was a bit misleading because it showed no US examples. In the US, there have been ample losses in trading accounts, but one would have to say it wasn't so much due to rogue traders, but to rogue trading *departments*. JPMorgan Chase announced in 2012, that they—a federally insured bank—had lost $6 billion on trading their own account. JPMorgan's trading account is four times the size of BofA's, despite having only about 10% more in assets.

A bank's most important liabilities are to its depositors, but those are not the only ones. The liabilities constitute everything the bank owes to anyone.

**Deposits**  The dollar amount that the bank owes to its depositors. In bank balance sheets, this is often broken out into interest-bearing and non-interest-bearing accounts, to give a first-approximation guess at the bank's cost of funds. You can use this to compute the *loan to deposit ratio* for a bank. It's just what it sounds like, the dollar volume of loans divided by the dollar volume of deposits, and the higher the value, the higher the risk. According to 2011 FDIC data, banks generally run in the 75-85% range, though they are commonly up in the 90s, too. The banks in the table are at 101%, 91%, and 71%, respectively. Bank of America has lots of lending capacity by this measure, and Washington Trust looks pretty much tapped out. BND (page 32) is at 65%. The Sunnydale bank, as we originally drew it on page 19, was at 105%. Obviously this is possible, but there has to be some reasoning why it's not a big risk.

**Federal funds purchased & repo agreements**  This is just the flip side of the same kinds of transactions as you see on the Asset side of the accounting. Here, the bank is borrowing the funds. From a bank's perspective (or the bank examiner's) the important aspect of borrowing through these transactions is that they are free of reserve requirements. A bank can lend and borrow in the Fed funds and repo markets without affecting the reserves it is required to have on hand, which is why they have their own line on the balance sheet. This means a bank can borrow in those markets to make up a reserve shortfall, often why such loans are made.

**Trading liabilities**  Like the trading assets, the trading liabilities are supposedly only relevant to the bank's "own" money. Just to pick a not-so-random example, JPMorgan Chase's trading assets of $314 billion minus their trading liabilities of $118 billion is larger than their capital of $142 billion. In other words, it is fairly obvious that they are actually trading with money they owe to others, though they doubtless have rulings and arguments from their teams of attorneys to claim otherwise.[26]

In addition to these, the bank probably has some unpaid suppliers, sick time it owes its employees, other forms of loans it has taken, and so on.

Turning to the capital, again, this is whatever the bank has and doesn't owe to anyone: the bank equity capital, or equity. The two components are the stock it has sold over the course of its existence and whatever profit it has made and not distributed to its shareholders: what it was given and what it earned itself.

**Stock** This is the dollar value of the stock issued by the bank. When you're calculating how much of a company you own, the nominal value (*par value*) of the stock is what's relevant.[27] The total stock of Washington Trust is $3 million. If you owned $300,000 of shares, you would own 10% of that bank, even if you bought them for $500,000. If the stock has no par value, then this is just the market value of the stock.

**Surplus** This is the amount of capital there is beyond the nominal value of the shares. There are a few different ways for it to get into the balance sheet. One way is that when the bank stock was sold to the public, the surplus is how much beyond the par value that the bank actually got for its shares. That $3 million in Washington Trust shares actually sold for $175,241,000, probably in several sales over the years. Not all stock has a par value. At RBS Citizens, the balance sheet has only $1,000 in common stock and $75,000 in preferred stock, probably because it's a subsidiary of the Royal Bank of Scotland. In those cases, the "surplus" is the whole value of the stock, and voting and ownership rights are figured in some other way. Again, the distinction is only important because the nominal dollar value of your stock is how you tell how much of a company you own.

---

[26]Part of that, of course, is the legacy of the brokerage part of Bear Stearns, which Morgan now owns. Unfortunately, they still have FDIC insurance, so what they *were* is not as important as what they *are*: a bank engaged in risky investments using explicit federal insurance as well as the implicit guarantee of being Too Big To Fail.

[27]In the tables here, this counts both perpetual preferred stock and common stock, something that will be appalling to accounting purists, but the distinction is irrelevant here.

If there is no par value for a stock, the surplus will be whatever the difference is between the other components of capital and the liabilities and the assets. It is sometimes difficult to ascribe a real meaning to the number, which might be
the result of lots of different accounting decisions over the
bank's history.

Not surprisingly for an alternative institution, the Bank of
North Dakota has an alternative definition of surplus. In
the 1970s, when the North Dakota legislature wanted to put
money into the BND to increase its capital, they called that
additional capital "surplus," apparently just to have a place
to account for it on the balance sheet.[28]

**Retained profits** Anything the bank has earned and not distributed as dividends to its shareholders belongs to the bank
and doesn't have to be paid to anyone. Therefore it counts as
capital. You can see some very different business strategies
here. BND is wholly owned by the state of North Dakota,
who started it in 1919 but put little money into it after that
(except for that period in the 1970s). So almost all its capital
is retained earnings. Washington Trust also has a fairly high
proportion of its capital in retained earnings, while it makes
up only about 10% of the capital for the two bigger banks
in table 2.1. These banks have earned plenty of profit, but it
has likely been distributed to their shareholders.[29]

# Leverage

Archimedes said that with a lever long enough he could move
the world. Though we'll never know where he thought he could
put the fulcrum, he was right that a lever is a great way to amplify
force. In finance, *leverage* means amplifying funds by using a small
amount of money to reap the benefit of investing a large amount of

---

[28]With the added benefit that future legislatures would not really have a claim
on it, as they do have on retained profit.

[29]In 2007 and 2008, as the sub-prime mortgage crisis mounted, the biggest
banks in the US were allowed to make dividend payments roughly equivalent to
half the amount of the TARP payments used to bail them out in the fall of 2008. No
regulators persuaded them (let alone forced them) to beef up their capital position,
either in the face of the mounting storm, or *even after it had struck.*

money. When someone makes a cash down payment on a home, they are leveraging the cash they have with a bank loan. For the investors in a bank, by investing a relatively small amount (the startup capital), they have an institution that can attract deposits, and so have access to the returns made from investing all the assets, a much larger number. The Sunnydale Bank investors own only $100 million, but have developed access to a billion dollars of investable funds. This leverage is how they can get a 15% return on their equity from loans that pay only 3%.

When you hear people talk about a bank's *leverage ratio*, they're talking about comparing the invested capital (the equity) to the total assets. For the Bank of Sunnydale, the leverage ratio would be a little less than 10%. Because what we usually want is a measurement of the level of risk a bank's management has taken on, this is frequently reported as a ratio between Tier 1 capital and assets. A ratio with invested capital will show you how profitable a bank is, but that is usually of more interest to people buying shares than to regulators. In the sample balance sheets on page 31 you can see that BofA has a leverage ratio around 12.4%.[30]

Leverage can produce amazing outcomes and is how some colossal fortunes were built, but the tricky thing about financial leverage is that it works quite well in reverse. That is, you can use leverage to build a colossal fortune, but you can also use it to destroy one—or several.

Remember the Sunnydale Bank? Imagine that, with capital equal to 10% of their assets, they had 5% of their loans go bad. The loan losses come out of capital, so that loss would be almost *half* their capital That's terrible news, but the bank will survive, because they still have the other half. They'll live, potentially to look for new capital (presumably from people who enjoy rollercoaster rides). But suppose their capital was only equal to 5% of their assets? In that case, the same loan loss would wipe them out

---

[30]This is only for the BofA subsidiaries whose balance sheets are in the FDIC data, see table 2.1. BofA as a whole has a substantially lower leverage ratio of about 10.7%, and when you restrict the leverage calculation to the Tier 1 capital, the number is about 7.5%, somewhat below its peer group average of 9.5%, according to the Bank Holding Company Performance Report (BHCPR) available at www.ffiec.gov. What this tells you is that while BofA contains bank subsidiaries being run conservatively, the overall company is highly leveraged and therefore fairly risky. Since the whole company is supported by being too big to fail, this additional risk is supported by taxpayers, even though it's apparently not risk borne by any part of the insured subsidiaries.

and leave them selling the CEO's jets on eBay to make good their debts. In other words, a bank leveraged to 5% is vulnerable if only one loan in 20 goes bad. That's not an outlandish loss to expect, but it would wipe out *all* the investors' capital.

For a banker, the important thing about leverage is that increasing it (which is equivalent to *decreasing* the leverage ratio) is how a bank can make a lot of money. For a regulator, the important thing about leverage is that increasing it is how a bank can lose a lot of money. A bank with a lot of capital and little leverage is far less vulnerable to all kinds of risks than a bank with a small amount of capital and lots of leverage. Remember, as we saw in "Accounting for risk" on page 27, that a bank's capital structure is just one source of risk. A "risky" bank with capital equal to only 1% of its assets can still be safe if all the money is invested in T-bills. Conversely, a bank with capital equal to 50% of its assets can still be risky if its assets are all speculative oil and gas leases or loans to poker players. Proposals to increase capital requirements in order to increase the security of banks can be counter-productive if they don't address the composition of the assets. There are lots of proposals out there to make the global financial network less risky, but the bottom line is that unless they involve reducing the permissible levels of leverage *and* addressing the risk inherent in a bank's assets, they probably don't amount to real change.

# Alternatives to fractional reserve banking

You will sometimes hear about *fractional reserve banking* but this only means the case where a bank takes in deposits and loans most of it out again, reserving only a small percentage to handle the daily demand for customer withdrawals. This is, of course, exactly the process we've been describing, and is how all the known banks in the world currently work. However, there are a variety of ways in which people who feel uncomfortable with the concept have sought to modify or disguise it.

## Islamic banking

The Koran forbids usury[31] and in order to have an economy at all, Islamic scholars have come up with ways to arrange things to satisfy the dictates of that religion, commonly referred to as *Islamic banking*. In practice, these are mostly just restrictions on destructive banking practice and new names for familiar concepts. For example, you might see a *buy-back agreement* instead of a loan. In exchange for a fee, a bank might buy a house for you and lease it to you in a lease-to-own arrangement. One way to look at this is so say the flows of money from you to the bank and from the bank to the seller are nearly the same as in a conventional mortgage loan, but called by different names. In the example of the home buyer, the payments made on the house might be a "lease payment" instead of a payment of principal and interest on a loan.[32] You could draw a block diagram of the flows of money for an Islamic bank and it would look identical to a conventional bank, but the labels on the arrows would be different.

Where Islamic banking does part company with conventional banks (at least in theory) is in the inclusion of a moral code behind the business. The relationship between debtor and creditor is, at bottom, ruled by conceptions of morality. Grim experience tells us that in what passes for the ethical code that dominates in the American banking industry today, there is apparently little room for conceptions of responsibility to one's customers or community. The simple code that appears to dominate is that debtors are bad people if they don't pay back their loans and creditors are bad people if they don't use every advantage to make money from their customers.

The Islamic scholars who interpret the Koran to set out rules of banking have a different perspective, and have come up with rules about how being a morally upright banker requires not exploiting the customer, and sharing the risk of making investments in the future. The idea is that the bank is to be more of a partner

---

[31]The Bible does too, for that matter (both testaments). However, over the centuries, the Christian world has shifted from a strict observance of that prohibition—where Jews were the only ones permitted to lend money—to a much less strict version, to none at all. The conservative branches of Islam, by contrast, have moved in the opposite direction, and many of the innovations of Islamic banking are actually 20th century developments.

[32]A buy-back agreement is the same idea as a repo transaction (see page 64), but those are cast as sales in order to avoid regulatory, not divine, condemnation.

with its customer, aiming to provide growth with equity, not just a creditor demanding a return on its money. These are interesting conceptions of banking, and though it is difficult to say whether real Islamic banks today honor those strictures, it's relatively easy to say that the conventional banking industry could benefit from a similarly rigorous examination of what morality means in the industry.

## Full reserve banking

You'll occasionally hear people talk about *full reserve banking* or *100% reserve banking*. These terms encompass a proposal for a new kind of bank, not a description of a bank that exists. Lending some or most of the money you deposit still happens in such a bank, but it's made somewhat more explicit to the depositor by making it clear that deposit accounts of one sort will be lent out while others will be kept as cash. There is much to be said for making the depositor more aware of the risks and benefits of what happens to his or her money, but one of the functions of a bank is to render long-term loans out of short-term deposits. (Academics call this the *maturity transformation* function of a bank.) No one wants to deposit money into a 30-year CD, but 30 years is a standard term for a mortgage. It's possible to finagle a way around this, but to the extent you create a 100%-reserve bank whose accounting solves this problem, you've created something that looks very much like a conventional bank, only with somewhat different labels for the same activities.

In short, while in a theoretical sense, there might be other models for banking, they are not in practice now.[33] "Fractional reserve banking" is just "banking" in the real world.

---

[33]The "shadow" banks that helped bring us the financial meltdown in 2008 might be an exception. These institutions, many of them also known as the nation's investment banks, had no reserve requirements for the derivative investments they were selling. Some customer would buy a share of some pile of derivative investments, and Goldman Sachs, or Lehman, or Bear Stearns, or whoever sold it, could turn around and use *all* of that money to invest in something else, like a short sale of that same security. As we know now, (a) they often did exactly that, and (b) this did not turn out well for anyone except the executives whose idea it was.

*Three*

# Bank operation made simple(r)

A BANK AND THE REVENUE STREAMS that support it do not just spring into existence on day one. It takes effort to find deposits and effort to lend them out. Few banks open up with loan customers on the doorstep with good business ideas, or deposit customers strolling in the door looking for a place to deposit their money. Why do banks offer free toasters and tablets for new accounts? Because they need to. Why do banks offer teaser loan rates? Because they need to.

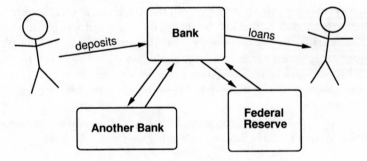

*Figure 3.1: Don't be fooled. Diagrams like this tell a story, but they only tell a tiny bit of it. Simplified boxes and arrows are easy to draw, but they can hide much more than they reveal.*

This is all merely to say that if you're going to think about banking in a productive way, you can't just look at the block diagram, the circles and arrows that indicate the flow of money. There is a lot hiding under those arrows and mastering block diagrams and balance sheets isn't the same as understanding the issues bankers face each day. Managing the different types of risk, types of lending, and the relationship to other banks are all important parts of starting a bank and keeping it going.

# Bank income

The varieties of ways banks generate money is staggering. Of course, the basics have only to do with the classic investment advice: buy low, sell high. Banks take money in at a low interest rate and lend it out at a higher rate, and that's all.[34] Pretty dull, right? Savings and loans were once known as the "3-6-3" business: take money in a 3%, loan it out at 6%, be on the golf course by 3 o'clock. That's all changed, not necessarily for the better.

Especially with the decline in interest rates over the past decade, banks increasingly have turned to fee income. This isn't just the kinds of fees like you pay on a checking account or on credit cards, though it certainly includes those. It's also fees on business like trust management, brokerage, bond issuances.

Of course there is a chicken-and-egg effect here. Rates can be so low only because banks have all this fee income built into their business model. Banks can be profitable with almost zero interest rates, particularly when the Federal Reserve lets them borrow at those rates. In an earlier climate, banks would be begging the Fed for higher rates long before this point. Even now, though, smaller banks, who tend not to have the fee income of the larger ones, are suffering.

Here's a short and incomplete list of the many ways banks make money besides interest rate arbitrage.

**Financial Advice** Banks frequently offer financial advice to their customers, and charge for the privilege of receiving that advice.

---

[34]This is also called interest rate *arbitrage*, a fancy word that just means taking advantage of a difference in price between two markets. A bank with a global reach can notice that some bond is selling for one price in London and for a lower price in Tokyo. If they can act quickly enough, they can buy in Tokyo and sell in London and make a bundle before the price difference disappears. This is bond price arbitrage. In almost the same way, interest rates are usually quite different in the market for loans and the market for deposits.

**Trust service** A *trust* is an independent entity with some assets or an income stream to manage. The trust department of some bank might be available either to be the trustee or just to manage the assets under the oversight of some outside trustee. Lots of bond transactions will require a trust of some kind, perhaps to receive some income stream on behalf of the bond owners, or to oversee paying down some previously issued bond.

**Fund management** Banks don't just give advice, they frequently manage investment funds, too. This is often in conjunction with some other service, like trust management, but by no means always. Fees are usually assessed as a percentage of the funds under management.

**Letters of credit** For a fee, a bank will commonly offer its reputation, its credit rating, for a customer who needs to buy something on credit. The LOC assures the seller that payment will be forthcoming, so it's ok to ship. LOCs are also used in loan transactions to substitute the bank's credit rating for the (presumably not as good) borrower's credit rating. This allows the borrower to borrow at a lower rate. Unfortunately, LOCs have a term, which is usually much shorter than the bond term, which means they have to be renewed, at which time the bank has a certain amount of leverage over the borrower.

**Bond sales** This is more of an investment bank function, but many big banks now have sister investment banks within the same holding company. A government or company that wants to issue bonds generally has them purchased by some bank for resale on the open market. This bank is the *underwriter* of a bond. The bank will build some profit into the transaction, sometimes in obvious ways, sometimes not. Banks are sometimes both the financial advisor to some city or town and the underwriter of its bonds. This is an obvious conflict of interest, but has been the order of the day for some time, since the wall between investment banks and commercial banks was punctured by the repeal of the Glass-Steagall act in the 1990s. The Dodd-Frank legislation was supposed to have clarified this, but that bill remains a work in progress.

**Sales of loans** A bank makes a loan, and then it has an asset that produces income. At some future time, it might decide to sell that asset to someone else. This will give it more capital with which it can make more loans, or invest in some other way.[35]

**Payment processing** A bank charter is essentially permission to transform checks into money and the other way around. Lots of money market funds exist that are not part of some bank. These funds will need this kind of service, which is why the checks for a fund you might own typically don't have the fund company's name on them, but some bank's instead.

**Lockbox service** A government, agency, or company that sends out bills and receives payments, can use a *lockbox service* to receive the funds. This is an address to which customers send their bill payments, and the bank facilitates turning those payments into account balances.

**Consumer fees** Fee income from bank account customers has become increasingly important to banks. This includes the familiar account maintenance fees, ATM fees, overdraft fees, money transfer fees, and so on. Banks also charge merchants a fee when they take a debit card in a transaction.[36]

**Credit card processing** A credit card customer is essentially a borrower and so pays interest on his or her balance, but even customers who pay off their balance each month are subject to a variety of fees: late fees, annual fees, over-the-limit fees, and more. The most notorious is the *swipe fee*, also called the *interchange fee*, charged to merchants who accept a card

---

[35] As will be blindingly obvious to virtually anyone who reads this far, the secondary market for loans is a big deal and is intimately related to the sad history of the 2007-08 financial crisis, but it's worth remembering that there are perfectly sound reasons both for selling loans *and* for constructing mortgage-backed bonds in order to do so. The fact that both of these were abused during the run-up to the crisis in no way diminishes their utility as a vehicle for policy.

[36] Reducing or eliminating those fees was supposed to be part of the Dodd-Frank legislation to establish the Consumer Financial Protection Bureau, but the rules that came out of the legislation weren't as effective, so customers currently pay an average of 24 cents per transaction while the cost to the banks is closer to 5 cents according to a 2013 report from the Fed.

for payment. Swipe fees for credit cards earn banks over $30 billion each year, in the US alone.[37]

**Restating value of assets** Other traditional ways for a bank to "make" money involve fiddling with the accounting. For example, a bank can appear to make money by decreasing its loan loss reserve. This increases the value of the assets, which is compensated for by increasing the value of the re- tained profits on the other side of the balance sheet. And, of course, such profits don't have to be retained and can be distributed as dividends, or bonuses. Other ways to have the same effect involve getting real property re-appraised, changing the risk model, or simply claiming a higher value for the assets, perhaps because of market changes, or per- haps because someone in accounting was suborned.

This is really only the beginning of the ways banks find to earn income. Each of the categories above has sub-categories, and doubtless there are entire categories that have been overlooked.

# Managing bank risk

A bank's operation is all about taking risks and managing them,[38] but there are several different kinds of risk: credit risk, liquidity risk, market risk, concentration risk, regulatory risk, operational risk. And tornadoes. Considering the different kinds of risk will help make sense of the purpose behind the various regulatory ra- tios and rules and also help refine your sense of what kinds of activities are wise for a bank to undertake.

---

[37]Merchants in the US pay very high swipe fees compared to other countries, an average of 2% of each transaction. In Great Britain, swipe fees are around 0.79% and the European Union limits them to 0.3% of each transaction. In 2012, a $7.3 bil- lion settlement was negotiated to settle a class-action antitrust suit that accused Visa and MasterCard of collusion and price-fixing their swipe fees. As of this writ- ing, the settlement is under attack by the merchants who call it inadequate, and it's not clear whether it will stand.

[38]Hopefully small and manageable risks, but as we've seen, not always. The difference between banks that go under and banks that do not is largely a matter of degree of risk, even if bankers will deny it.

- *Credit risk* is the most basic kind of bank risk. Give someone a loan, and they might not pay it back. The fear of this risk typically determines the interest rate a debt incurs. A risky debtor will only get a loan at a high rate.

- A bank's *liquidity risk* is the risk that it might not have enough cash on hand for customers who want their money back. Maybe it loaned too much out, or maybe too many loans went bad. A bank without plenty of cash on hand to serve its customers' needs has lots of liquidity risk. A *run* on a bank—when customers want money back that the bank doesn't currently have—is a liquidity crisis.

- A bank undertakes *market risk* when market conditions might change the value of some asset it owns. For example, if a bank holds $10 million in California state bonds, and the ratings agencies decide that California's credit rating is too high, the value of that asset might go down to $9 million. Another example would be that when real estate values drop, the value of the collateral a bank holds for its real estate lending falls. This will make the value of the loan itself fall. In both cases, the value of the bank's assets changed because of circumstances far beyond the bank's control, though obviously there was discretion involved in taking the risk in the first place.[39]

- Say you're a bank and took some deposits, promising to pay 1% interest. You used the money to make some long-term loans paying 3%. A couple of years down the road, interest rates rise, and your customers demand higher interest rates than a measly 1%. If you don't pay those higher rates, they'll withdraw their money and you'll have a liquidity crisis when you run out of cash. But if you pay your depositors 4%, then your cost of funds will be higher than what you're earning on your loans, and you'll lose money. Or maybe

---

[39]The mother of all market risks was, of course, the phenomenal bets banks made on subprime mortgage backed securities in the run-up to the financial crisis of 2008. When subprime mortgages went sour in large numbers, the market for these bonds evaporated nearly overnight. Some of the nation's largest banks still have billions of dollars of these bonds on their books, with essentially zero market value. A special exception to the accounting rules was granted by the Fed to keep banks like Bank of America, JPMorgan Chase, and Citigroup from being declared insolvent.

you bought a bunch of long-term Treasury securities as collateral, but then interest rates rise and the value of the collateral falls. In each case, your bank was overtaken by *interest rate risk*, a category of market risk that bankers often mention. Banks can be vulnerable to interest rate movements in either direction, depending on how it conducts its business. The debacle of the Philadelphia interest-rate swaps was a motivated by banks looking to offload interest-rate risk onto the city government.

- A bank that loans to too few customers (or takes deposits from too few) suffers from *concentration risk*. If something goes bad for a single one of your customers, do you want to risk your bank? Some customers, such as governments, may not be risky, but advocates for one-customer banks must be prepared to say why not.

- Banks can suffer from *regulatory risk*, when rules and regulations change, sometime without warning.[40]

- And *operational risk* is when something else goes wrong: software glitches, lost records, customers suing over deposit slip paper cuts, embezzlement and robbery,[41] executives jailed for wrongful foreclosures,[42] and so on. Technically speaking, tornadoes would actually fall under operational risk.

Different sets of customers and circumstances can present very different kinds of risks. Some customers have highly predictable

---

[40]Old Stone Bank in Rhode Island, a conservatively-run community bank (whose advertisements used to feature Fred Flintstone as spokesman), died when federal bank regulators asked them to take over two failed thrifts and a few months later changed their mind about the exceptions to the capital requirements they had made. Old Stone was liquidated and the shareholders sued the government for breach of contract. They won, but years too late to matter.

[41]The 1991 banking crisis in Rhode Island (see footnote, page 150) was triggered by the failure of Heritage S&L, a $22 million bank whose president, Joseph Mollicone, had embezzled $13.8 million, almost *two-thirds* of the entire bank. Needless to say, he became a fugitive from justice when state bank examiners finally noticed. (Until then, the bank had been "regulated" by a private insurer whose vice president was Mollicone himself.) He fled to Salt Lake City, where he bought a condo and lived comfortably for a year and a half before returning to RI and turning himself in to the state attorney general (in person) because he missed his mother.

[42]Just kidding, that last one doesn't really happen, even though tens of thousands of people have been robbed of their homes this way.

cash flows, for example. For these customers, liquidity risk is easy to manage, and so a bank's cash reserves can be lower. Remember, the regulatory minimum for reserves is just that, *a minimum*. Prudent management can, and often does, require higher reserves for certain classes of customers. Another bank might find itself lending to highly reliable customers, but with a very unpredictable source of funds. For example, it might be funding its lending operation by borrowing in the repo market. This bank has to tread carefully, because even though its credit customers are very reliable, the interest rate on its borrowing can change rapidly.

A bank can, and should, be aware of the risks on its balance sheet, and ought to do whatever it can to minimize them. At some level, the risks are unavoidable, so the bank must insure itself against them, but for several kinds of risk, there are reasonable measures to take against them. Being alert to borrowers who may be in trouble is one obvious step to take, as is managing collateral to maximize its value. A bank can reduce its liquidity risk through analysis of its deposit customers in order to understand the ebb and flow of their deposits. A bank can reduce its market risk by spreading its investments around into a variety of different venues.

The other way to manage risk, of course, is to find someone else to take it, wittingly or not. A great deal of life in America today can usefully be viewed as a struggle about who assumes risk. Who, for example, assumes the risk that an air traveler suffers a family emergency that prevents travel? Is the lost fare the traveler's problem, or the airline's? The airlines used to assume that risk, but not so much any more. Bus lines now sell reserved seats instead of open-ended tickets, reducing the risk of empty buses (or over-full ones), but increasing the risk to the traveler that he or she will not be able to use the ticket. Health insurers sell large-deductible policies where someone who gets ill can be liable for thousands of dollars in medical costs. Consumer products companies make customers pay for a warranty that once was considered a selling point. The consumer can gripe about having to assume risk that once was invisible, but risk is a real thing. If you wait long enough, any risk will cause a loss. Companies can only absorb so much risk before they can endure no more. The struggle, or negotiation if you prefer, is about determining where that line is between an acceptable sharing of risk and an unconscionable shirking of it.

These same motives push banks. Is an interest-rate swap like Philadelphia's a way to accommodate the differing needs of the two parties, or a way for a bank to foist interest-rate risk onto an unsuspecting customer? Is mortgage securitization the way Indy-Mac and Lehman Brothers (and so many others) do it a way to increase the pool of money available to a bank, or a way to foist credit risk onto bondholders? Is a CD a convenient way to get a higher interest rate or a way to get a bank's customers to assume some of its liquidity risk?

# Lending

When banks lend, they look for liquidity, security, and yield. Like the joke about good, fast, and cheap, you can get generally get any two qualities out of three, but no more. Often, you have to make do with just one.

For example, T-bills—very short-term loans to the US government—are very liquid and very secure,[43] but also have about the lowest yields around, measurable in units of hundredths of a percent (also called *basis points*). Or you could look for security and yield, and offer 30-year mortgages, where the yield is higher, and security is decent (if you're careful with your lending standards), but they aren't nearly as liquid. Or you could opt for liquidity and yield—certain "tranches" of mortgage-backed bonds (see "Subdividing bonds" on page 135) were quite liquid and quite profitable during the 2002–2006 period—but those investments were pretty risky, as the catastrophe of 2008 showed.

A bank's loan portfolio has to balance all three of these qualities. It's not good enough to have a collection of really secure loans if the bank will suffer a liquidity crisis before they're paid back. Similarly, it's not much use to make only very liquid and secure investments if operating costs will sink the bank because its assets have such low yields. Because the world ultimately is not very predictable, a little humility is in order while making that design. A bank whose solvency depends on everything turning out just right won't convince the regulators (and maybe investors, or legislators) who need to be convinced.

---

[43]Despite the efforts, near the time of this writing, by Republicans in the US House of Representatives to threaten default on those obligations.

## Lending theory

It's well and good to put up balance sheets to talk about, but it's also worth looking at the process by which they change. Let's imagine the Bank of Sunnydale just about to make its first loan. You can see its balance sheet for its initial condition on page 22.

Let's assume that before anyone shows up with money to deposit that a fine and credit-worthy customer named Henry is at the door on day one wanting to borrow a million dollars. Because Sunnydale's management is young and foolish and because it suits our pedagogical purpose to say so, Henry's loan application is approved instantly. Sunnydale management pays the loan by establishing an account for Henry, and their balance sheet now looks like this:

| Assets | Liabilities & Capital |
|---|---|
| $1 million loans | $1 million deposits |
| $10 million building, artwork | |
| $5 million intangibles | $0 retained profits |
| $30 million securities | $30 million stock |
| $5 million cash | $20 million surplus |
| $51 million | $51 million |

Sunnydale has simply made up the money in Henry's account, and balances it with the asset represented by the pile of loan agreements Henry filled out in order to get the loan. Nothing else on the balance sheet changes. In a way there is something slightly magical about this—the bank has appeared to create money out of nothing—but what happens when Henry wants to spend his loan proceeds?

Suppose Henry writes a check for $1 million and gives it to Sarah in exchange for a lovely mansion and estate in Sunnydale's suburbs. Sarah deposits the check in her bank who submits it for clearing and the result is a message that tells Sunnydale to transfer $1 million to Sarah's bank *and* to debit Henry's account for the funds. The money transferred could be cash, though it is more likely to be deposits in Sunnydale's account at some other bank, like the Fed. So they execute the transfer and now Sunnydale's balance sheet looks like this:

| Assets | Liabilities & Capital |
|--------|----------------------|
| $1 million loans | $0 deposits |
| $10 million building, artwork | |
| $5 million intangibles | $0 retained profits |
| $30 million securities | $30 million stock |
| $4 million cash | $20 million surplus |
| $50 million | $50 million |

The books stay balanced because we've deducted the same amount from the deposits as from the "cash" line of the assets. Later, as Henry pays back his loan, his payments will decrease the outstanding value of his loan, increase the "cash" line on the assets side of the sheet, and also increase the "retained profits" line in the capital with the part of his payments that represent the interest.

This transfer of funds has changed Sunnydale's balance sheet, but not in a bad way. They still have enough reserves for what they need to do, which is to attract deposits and loan customers. But what would have happened if Sarah's check had left the cash reserves below the minimum reserves for their deposits? In that case, Sunnydale would have had to do something to increase its reserves. There are a lot of choices, including buying more toasters to attract more new depositors, selling some securities, borrowing in the Fed funds market, pledging securities for a repo loan, selling some artwork, bidding for funds in the large CD or Eurodollar market, selling more bank stock, selling their financial advice, leasing some of their intangible property, lying about their revenues to get a tax refund, whatever. The choice they make is a management decision; what matters to the compliance department is that the reserves return to an adequate level. What matters to the shareholders is that this be done in a sustainable and at least moderately intelligent fashion. Some shareholders may care whether it is legal, too.

## Lending reality

An important point about lending is that arranging a loan and the legal documents surrounding a loan takes time and effort. Finding loan customers takes time and persuading them to work with you takes time. Even filling out loan agreements takes time. Bank investors and examiners routinely say that it takes at least three years to turn a new bank (also commonly referred to as a *de novo* bank) into a profitable concern because that's how long it takes to arrange loans of all the money.[44]

To a certain extent the logistics of making loans is how the really big banks become detached from their communities. In today's economy, little local banks are more likely to have a full loan portfolio than the big banks (as in the table on page 31). There are many pressures on banks to grow: the yields on bonds and other financial products get much better with a bigger pool of money to invest, and there are regulatory economies of scale. If you're earning some of your bank's income through fees, a larger customer base will produce more fees, and so on.

Unfortunately, one place where economies of scale can't necessarily work out is in the management of a loan portfolio. Just because a loan portfolio is large doesn't mean that the average size of a loan is large. A loan portfolio ten times bigger than another might require at least ten times as many loan officers to manage it all. A bank whose management expects to see economies of scale in their lending operation will be forced to seek ever-larger opportunities, which turn out to be precisely the opportunities that shrink the fastest in an economic downturn.[45]

What this means is that a very large bank can seldom afford to pursue any but the most routine small loans along with its really big ones. Real estate loans are generally quite routine, and denominated in the six figures. Business loans, especially lines of credit, can be substantially smaller than the mortgage on a typical house, and the loan approval process is much more complicated. Lending to a business means you have to understand that business, which can be much more challenging than understanding the real estate market. This means that small businesses tend to get the cold shoulder from the biggest banks, exactly what we've seen over the past few years.

---

[44]Another way to say this is that many bank business plans foresee three (or more) years of losses before they get to the profits, something to keep in mind while you're trying to sell your idea to someone. This is not to say it's impossible to come up with a design that's profitable on day one, but people in the industry tend not to expect that.

[45]Other potential strategies are to automate loan approvals, removing the subjective judgment of people who know the borrowers from the process, and to outsource the whole problem to mortgage brokers who really don't care at all. Big banks engaged in both strategies with zeal 2000–2007 and both played an important role in the mortgage disaster that triggered the financial crisis of 2008.

According to statistics from the Federal Reserve, *community banks*—banks with less than $10 billion in assets—make up only 20% of the bank deposits in America, but half of the business lending. Those small banks are the ones who feel the pressure to understand their local businesses and so can feel comfortable extending credit there.

You might consider starting a bank to push back against this tendency, maybe by making business lending—or facilitating business lending—one of its core functions. Still, even a bank with that goal can't change the fact that it takes work to move money out the door.[46] The financial projections you make to justify the creation of such a bank have to account for this time, and you need a strategy for paying the bills after opening the doors and before achieving profitability.

## Bankers and bond basics

There are borrowers out there far too big for any bank to handle. Governments and large corporations frequently need to borrow amounts in the tens or hundreds of millions, or more, too big for most banks to handle. Other large borrowers might want a loan within the capacity of a bank, but feel they don't want to agree to the kinds of restrictions a bank will put on its loans. Both categories of borrowers can turn to the bond market, and sell a *bond*— a long-term, resellable, liability—to willing investors.[47] Bond buyers (the lenders) include banks, but also insurance companies and institutional investors, like foundations and pension funds. Individuals buy them as well, for secure savings, either individually, or through mutual funds.

The existence of the bond market makes highly-rated bonds a fairly liquid investment, even if they have a long term. If you hold a bond and want to turn that asset into cash, you can sell it to someone else. You'll lose the interest you would have gotten if you'd held the bond to term, but the price you sell it at will probably allow you to keep most of the interest accrued to

---

[46]This highlights one of the potential advantages of a bank whose customer base includes governments: they are large debtors. The scale and predictability of a government's borrowing needs imply that a public bank able to underwrite government borrowing might be able to fill out much of its loan portfolio in a much shorter time than another bank might.

[47]For more about the bonds themselves, see "Bonds and other borrowing" on page 128.

date. This makes bonds relatively safe investments. No investment is risk-free, and sometimes bonds aren't repaid (credit risk) and there can be considerable interest rate risk, especially with a long-term bond. That is, if you hold a 30-year bond at a 5% interest rate, the value of that bond will drop precipitately if interest rates rise to 6%.

Banks have a special position in the bond market, as it is often a bank who acts as the *underwriter* of a bond. (This is usually an investment bank's function, rather than a commercial bank's.) The underwriter (or underwriters, as the case may be) buys the bonds from the issuing company or government, and then offers them for resale to other buyers. The underwriter assumes the risk of selling the bond, so usually it only does so if it is also involved in other market activity, like trading securities, that bring it into contact with bond buyers.

Underwriters are often part of a syndicate, especially for bond issues that might be too large for an individual bank.

Sometimes a bank will buy an entire bond offering and just keep it. This is known as a *private placement* and is considered to be different from just a bank loan, though how exactly it differs is a matter of fine philosophical distinctions. The issuance costs are different, so there is a practical distinction, but that's a result, not a cause, or so they say.

To a significant extent, a fair amount of the evolution of banking over the past 40 years has been a reaction to the increasing accessibility of the bond market. Back when bonds were only available through the mediation of big banks, banks weren't really in competition with bond buyers to fund investment. Today, when a universe of bond dealers is out there, only some of whom are associated with banks, a bank is in direct competition with buyers in the bond market. Because there is so much money available for investment in bonds, this is no small part of the downward pressure on loan yields and bank profits.

## Money market lending

As we saw in the example balance sheets back in chapter 2, bank-originated loans are hardly the only items on the asset side of a bank's balance sheet. There is a universe of assets banks can earn money with out there.

Banks make up the largest part of the worldwide *money mar-*

*ket.* This is the name we use to refer to the market for relatively short-term sources of money. It's not a physical marketplace, and it encompasses a lot of different kinds of borrowing and lending, mostly between financial institutions, but governments and non-financial corporations also play a role, as do customers of money-market funds, a kind of mutual fund that invests in these highly liquid short-term securities.

The money market instruments used for lending from one bank to another are also used by banks to borrow from each other, so they are described in "Borrowing" on page 58. But banks are not the only players in the money market. Quite a bit of money market activity is on behalf of corporations and governments.

Short-term loans to companies are usually called *commercial paper*. These are unsecured bonds, sold on the open market, with a fixed maturity of less than nine months. Despite the lack of collateral, commercial paper is generally quite a good bet, since it's usually only the really credit-worthy customers who use this method of financing. A company with a poor credit rating will find commercial paper to be a very expensive way to get a loan, so they rely on other means to finance operations.

Governments use the money market to manage their cash flow, since tax funds ebb and flow during the course of a fiscal year, and the fluctuations don't necessarily coincide with the ebb and flow of their expenses. Governments will use the money market to cover short-term finance gaps. For example, a *tax anticipation note* (*TAN*) is a short-term bond issue, meant to provide cash before some tax payment is due. (A *note* is just jargon for a short-term bond.) A city that expects a surge of property-tax payments in August might issue a TAN in May to cover a few months' cash flow needs.

The federal government is a big user of short-term securities, which it uses to iron out the differences between getting and spending the funds it runs on. A Federal bond with a maturity of less than a year is called a *Treasury bill* or *T-bill*.[48]

There is more about bonds, bonding, and the bond markets in Chapter 6.

---

[48] A medium-term bond is a Treasury *note* and only the long-term stuff is actually called bonds. Who knows why? It's just jargon; do you feel like an insider yet?

## Secondary markets

A bank that has loaned all the money it feels safe to lend can make no more loans without securing some more money, somehow. It can increase its capital by selling stock or refraining from distributing profits. Depending on its capital ratios, it could choose instead to increase its liabilities, by increasing deposits or borrowing from other banks. (More to come about that in "Borrowing" on page 58.) Also depending on the regulatory ratios, a bank can seek to transform assets that cannot readily be loaned—like a loan already on the books—into assets that can be loaned, like cash.

For example, a bank managing $100 mllion dollars worth of mortgage loans might sell someone the right to receive the payments on those mortgages for $100 million minus some profit for the buyer. Assuming the borrowers continue to pay their mortgages, the buyer will get a profit in exchange for taking the risk of default off the bank's books. The bank, in turn, will get almost $100 million it can lend again.[49]

The loans can also be used to back up a bond: the bank establishes a trust of some kind to receive the mortgage payments from all the homeowners, and distribute them to the owners of the security. This is an *asset-backed bond*, or a *mortgage-backed bond*, and the process is called *securitization*. You'll also see bonds like this called a *collateralized debt obligation* or *CDO*.

The secondary market for mortgages in the US is dominated by the quasi-public *government-sponsored enterprises* (*GSE*) called Fannie Mae, Freddie Mac, and the government-owned Ginnie Mae.[50] These are institutions whose purpose is to set standards

---

[49]As with most of these transfers of risk, it's fairly important that the buyer understand that they are assuming some risk and that risk means occasionally you lose. The 2008 crisis was largely due to the fact that very risky bonds were being sold as risk-free, and they found their way into places where the level of risk was inappropriate to the level of being, well, stupid.

[50]The names come from their acronyms, more or less. Fannie Mae is the Federal Natonal Mortgage Association (FNMA), and Ginnie Mae is the Government National Mortgage Association (GNMA), and if you try to pronounce both of those acronyms, you'll get a rough approximation of their nicknames. Freddie Mac is actually the Federal Home Loan Mortgage Corporation (FHLMC) and its origin is a bit more mysterious. "Mac" is longtime industry shorthand for a mortgage corporation, but how the "FHL" part came to be pronounced "Freddie" is a mystery that awaits further investigation by linguistic historians. One theory is that it had to do with the original acronym in the 1970 enabling legislation. There are doubtless other theories, equally accurate.

and use bond market money to buy mortgages that conform to those standards, and roll them into guaranteed bonds. Fannie Mae was founded as a government entity as part of the National Housing Act of 1934, part of the New Deal, but was privatized in 1968. Freddie Mac was founded in 1970 more or less as a private competitor to the now-private Fannie. Ginnie Mae was created in 1968, essentially to be the repository of Fannie Mae's loans that were awkward to privatize. Their private state lasted until the financial crisis, when they were caught up in the madness of the real estate bubble. The government bailed them out, and they are run by a conservator now, with their future the subject of ongoing debate. Before the financial crisis, Fannie and Freddie saw significant and increasing competition from private issuers of mortgage bonds, which is partly what drove them to join their private-sector brethren in the mortgage madness. They were hardly innocents in that debacle, though they were late to the party. The fallout from the events of 2007 discouraged most of the other mortgage-bond issuers, and as of the end of 2012, the GSEs issue plus Ginnie Mae issue almost all the mortgage bonds issued in the country.

As we saw in the 2008 financial crisis, there are lots of ways for mortgage bonds to go wrong, but the bond market is a *very* large source of funds. Through misuse, fraud, and customer abuse, mortgage bonds have acquired a bad reputation, but there are several perfectly valid policy reasons to admire using that market to strengthen the position of local banks, the original purpose to the GSEs.

One of the gotchas involved in secondary markets is that the stuff that circulates is likely to be the least desirable for a bank to keep. This is essentially the banking equivalent of *Gresham's Law*, that predicts that only the least valuable examples of some commodity will circulate.[51] In a world of floating interest rates, it does not pay to be the bank holding the low-interest loan when rates rise, so those are often the ones banks sell first. The result is that the loans a bank tries to keep on its books are likely to be

---

[51]Gresham's law, among the only "laws" of economics that really merits the name, says that bad money drives out good, so that if you have two coins of the same face value, but one has more intrinsic value than the other, that one will disappear from circulation. This is why you can't find dimes older than 1964 in your pocket change, but there are still plenty of pennies older than that. The dimes were silver before 1964, so they've vanished from circulation and live in private hoards of silver coins, never to be spent.

less-risky floating rate loans, while the ones they try to sell will be fixed rate or floating-rate loans to poor credit risks.[52]

## Loan insurance

One way to reduce the credit risk of a loan is for a bank to get insurance for it, and have the risk assumed by (or at least shared with) the insurance company. In the US, a great number of residential mortgages are insured by the federal government, either through the Federal Housing Administration (FHA) or through the Veterans Administration (VA). There is also private mortgage insurance, which you'll see as *PMI* on loan documents. These all work more or less the same way. The insurance is paid for with either a monthly premium, or a premium amortized over the life of the loan, which comes to more or less the same thing. The rates differ depending on the insurer, as well as who and where the borrower is. In the event of a default, the insurer pays the bank the unpaid portion of the principal on the loan.

Mortgage insurance has an impact on the secondary market. Fannie Mae was set up to buy FHA-insured mortgages. Banks who make FHA mortgages know they can get them off their books by selling them to Fannie.[53] Even if the bank has no intention of doing so, a portfolio of FHA-insured loans would be significantly more liquid in the event of trouble down the road than a portfolio without the insurance.

# Borrowing

In order to lend money, you must have some. Banks start their operation with capital—money they own and don't owe to anyone—but leveraging that capital with other people's money is what

---

[52]Not that they always succeed; see also the sad tale of Lehman Brothers, in "Subdividing bonds" on page 135.

[53]This is more than just a detail. An innovative plan to finance energy-efficiency improvements to homes called *Property Assessed Clean Energy* loans, (*PACE loans*) was seriously wounded when the FHA said it would not insure mortgages on properties with PACE liens on them. Without FHA insurance, a bank can't sell to Fannie, and thus must either keep the loan on their books, or find some other route to sell it. In other words, such lending is significantly more risky than it would be if FHA would insure them. Some states have changed their laws to make PACE lending acceptable to the FHA, but Fannie and Freddie remain reluctant participants, as of 2014.

banking is all about. There are several different ways banks borrow money: from depositors, in the repo market, from (or through) the Fed, and several more. All of these together constitute the *money market*. Each source has different advantages and disadvantages, and the cost of funds to a bank varies significantly, too.

The different sources of funding also have different levels of interest rate risk and liquidity risk. Customer deposits, for example, flow inexorably, but slowly, toward higher interest rates. Repo loans react much more quickly to interest rate changes. Banks with a small number of sources of money will also suffer from a kind of concentration risk, where a single depositor pulling out might conceivably cause a catatrophic liquidity crisis.

Some of the sources for bank funding are only available to the biggest banks. A credit union, for example, isn't going to be trolling the deposit note market looking for million-dollar CD purchases, and a community bank is not likely to be a securities dealer. Still, these are the ways that banks find money to lend, and because opportunity presents itself to prepared minds, it behooves even the smallest bank to understand what the possibilities actually are.

## Managing deposits

A depositor trusting a bank with their money is among the most fundamental transactions a bank makes. A decent body of deposits is also about the most stable source of funding for a bank's operation.

A bank's deposits come in different forms. A term deposit, like a CD, is just like a loan, where you give the bank some money and they promise it back on some date in the future. A demand deposit, like a checking or savings account, is essentially also a loan to the bank, though with unusually demanding terms where the lender can get some or all of their money back whenever they want.[54]

---

[54]Some people make a point of the fact that it's not really "your" money after you put it into the bank. This is technically true, but doesn't matter much in the context of running a bank. You can think of a deposit as a loan to the bank, or you can think of it as a purchase of a liability. In truth, it doesn't really matter; what matters is that the depositor can get the money back, either when he or she wants it, or at the end of the deposit term, depending on the kind of account.

Deposits, of course, are not free for the bank. A bank pays interest to its depositors, and the cost of maintaining branches, tellers, the ATM network, all those toasters, and the rest have to be included in the cost to the bank of depositors' funds. Depending on how they do the analysis of their customers, a bank might conclude that the cost of funds from some branch is too high. A branch in a poor neighborhood, for example, might not attract many deposits, but will cost just as much to operate as a branch in a rich neighborhood. A branch in a neighborhood near some big employer might attracts lots of customers who will arrange for direct-deposit of their paychecks. That branch will cost less to staff than a branch where no one does. There are a lot of variables, and for many banks, the only way they discover them is by opening (and often closing) branches.[55]

Beyond the simple cost of the funds, the other important fact about deposits is that they are short-term money. People put money into a bank with the intention of taking it out again relatively soon. Banks can make long-term loans against money like this only because collectively, a body of deposits might not be as volatile as any individual's account. The volatility of customer accounts varies a lot between banks and even between the kinds of customers at a bank. A bank needs to keep around the reserves it needs to service its accounts or the regulatory minimum, *whichever is greater*. The regulatory minimum a bank needs to keep around in reserves is, after all, a minimum, and certain classes of customers might force a bank to keep around much more cash.

Imagine an employee credit union at some large company in Sunnydale. Let's call it the Acme Credit Union. Acme might see all its accounts surge 20% when paychecks are issued every Friday. Suppose it usually has a million dollars in deposits on Thursday, and then $1.2 million on Friday. Acme would be foolish to think that it only has to keep around 10% of the deposits it has on payday because more than that is going to flow out of its customers' accounts during the march to the next payday. If they only keep $120,000 around in reserves (10%), they'll be scram-

---

[55]This is not to say that a bank cannot work against these pressures. In a better world, banks would do exactly that, and there are plenty of strategies available for doing so: cooperating with commercial or non-profit entities already present in targeted neighborhoods, for example. The people who hope to create banks that do so need to understand what they are undertaking and whence come the headwinds they will face.

bling for another $80,000 in cash to meet customer demand before next Thursday. More likely they set their reserve requirements to handle the low ebb of their weekly fluctuation and manage from there.

Specialized consulting companies exist whose business is analyzing the ebb and flow of a bank's accounts and advising management on the optimal ways to manage their cash and customer accounts. These are difficult problems, and are part of the reason CDs are popular with banks. CDs have a term, so banks know the customer isn't going to demand their money before the term completes. CDs originated in the 1960s for large deposits with a rate that companies would negotiate with their local bank. The development was largely due to an exemption for large deposits in the interest-rate limits legally imposed on banks at the time. It was only in the 1980s that they began to be offered at smaller denominations to the general pubic. Though CDs are available to anyone with the minimum deposit now, the market for large CDs persists and is still an important part of the world's money market.

Another source of deposits is called *brokered deposits*. This is where a securities broker makes a large deposit in a bank, and sells shares of that deposit to its clients. With so little overhead (the broker is doing the marketing), this is a relatively inexpensive source of deposits to a bank, even if the interest rate is commonly somewhat higher than on normal consumer accounts. There is, however, a certain amount of concentration risk, since the broker winds up in control of a large block of deposits. In the US, FDIC rules restrict brokered deposits to well capitalized banks. Brokered deposits are central to some banks' business strategy: Morgan Stanley gets almost all its deposits in this fashion, and Goldman Sachs gets a high proportion that way, too. These banks don't have branches, but they still have deposits. Even banks with lots of branches and a broad customer base sometimes turn to them as a useful source of funds: BankAmerica and Citigroup make substantial use of them, though they represent only 5-7% of their deposits.

A growth in reliance on brokered deposits can be a sign of trouble in a bank, and this is more or less what sank IndyMac, who used brokered deposits for more than a third of their deposit base by 2008. Unfortunately for them, in early 2008, a ratings downgrade of bonds based on their loans dramatically affected their CRAR by increasing the risk weights used to value their assets. A

bank has to be "well-capitalized" by FDIC standards to participate
in the brokered deposit market, and the downgrade threatened to
cut them off from this source of funding. Losing access to this
market would have bled them for around $500 million per month.
Insolvency threatened to follow. IndyMac, with the cooperation of
their regulator, found a borderline-fraudulent fix by backdating a
transfer of capital from their parent company. But, as frequently
happens when insolvency threatens a bank, the threat was made
good shortly thereafter by a good old-fashioned bank run, complete with crowds of angry depositors in the bank lobbies.

## Fed funds and the discount window

Too much money on reserve can be as much of a burden as too
little. Let's look at Acme Credit Union again. Remember they
have deposits of $1 million every Thursday and $1.2 million on
Friday, payday at Acme Manufacturing, the company for whose
employees the credit union was formed.

Acme's troubles aren't over if it just arranges to have 10% of
its deposits on reserve on Thursday. Suppose they do that, and
have a reserve of $100,000 in cash and reserve deposits available
on Thursday. What do they do with the excess $200,000 they get
on Friday? Remember, reserves bear no (or little) interest, so not
investing this surge of funds is sort of like wasting it. Acme could
use it to buy some liquid investment like T-bills and then sell them
the next week, or time the maturities to align to its needs, but
that's complicated, and the commissions on the sales would be
expensive. Also, T-bills pay almost nothing in interest and really
are not very different from cash. Buying a CD from another bank
isn't really an option, since those are usually longer terms than a
few days.

The *Fed funds* market is where a bank first turns to cover reserve problems like Acme's. Fed funds are the reserve funds that
banks keep on deposit at the Federal Reserve, or at Fed member banks.[56] Loans of these funds to each other are the goods of
the Fed funds market. Loans are short-term and uncollateralized,
and regulators don't count them against a bank's reserve requirements, so they can be used to meet those requirements.

---

[56] Acme, being a credit union, is not a Fed member, but it probably has relationships with one or more partner banks who are.

A bank in Acme's position might arrange to have around $100,000 on reserve (cash and deposits at other banks) at any time, and manage the ebb and flow by lending in the Fed funds market. On Friday, when Acme expects $200,000 to flow into its accounts, Acme can offer almost all of that money immediately to other banks who might have a reserve shortfall. They'll keep around $20,000 to make sure they have 10% of their deposits on reserve at the end of the day, but can loan the other $180,000. During the course of the week, they'll spend down the $20,000 and the $180,000 will be repaid and that, too, will be paid out to customers making withdrawals. And they'll earn a little interest income from the banks to whom they've loaned the funds.

Acme could do it slightly differently, and keep only $80,000 on reserve, and make up the difference by lending *and borrowing* on the Fed funds market. They wouldn't have as much to lend each Friday, and they would probably have to borrow each Wednesday, but they'd have 20% less money in cash and reserve accounts. If they can find good investments for that money, it might be worth the added risk of the lower reserves. You might call this a more aggressive way to run a bank, but it's not an unusual one.[57]

A bank facing a reserve shortfall can also borrow at the Fed's *discount window*, where a member bank can borrow at very low interest rates. discount window loans are short-term, with terms ranging from overnight to a month or so. They are different from Fed funds loans by being secured loans, with collateral pledged in the form of securities of various kinds, or loans the bank has made. A bank can get *primary credit* if it is healthy, with minimal overhead. A less well-capitalized bank will get *secondary credit*, which comes with a bit more analysis and paperwork and a slightly higher interest rate. The Fed can also extend longer-term

---

[57] Aggression, you'll be shocked to learn, is not a trait unheard of in the executive suites of our nation's leading financial institutions. At an IMF meeting in 2011, Jamie Dimon, the CEO of JPMorgan Chase who was said to be known as "Mad Dog" on the high school soccer field, berated the governor of the Bank of Canada so thoroughly that the president of Goldman Sachs felt compelled to apologize on his behalf. The Canadian banker's offense? Suggesting that increasing capital requirements would be good for the banking system. Dick Fuld, CEO of Lehman Brothers when it expired, was called "The Gorilla" for his rampaging style. Kenneth Lewis, ex-CEO of BankAmerica, Angelo Mozilo, formerly of CountryWide Financial, and Franklin Raines, once head of Fannie Mae, are all frequently described as aggressive and competitive, and all three brought their banks low in the 2008 crisis due to serious overreach.

*seasonal credit* to banks that have seasonal fluctuations in their reserves, like a bank in a farm or resort community might.    The primary credit rate is called the *discount rate*.[58]   Because of the collateral, even though the interest rate is low, the cost of those funds is not zero. The discount window sounds good, but there are lower rates available in Fed funds, so it is really just where a bank goes when it needs to. Fed policy more or less discourages its use.

## Repo market

A bank has other sources of funds. A *repurchase agreement*, or *repo* is essentially a short-term collateralized loan, framed as two sales. (You'll also see it in banking documents as *RP* sometimes.) I borrow money from you by selling you some securities with an agreement that tomorrow you'll sell them back to me at a slightly higher price. I get the use of your money for a while and you get the securities as collateral. The higher price is calculated by adding the *repo rate*, the interest rate, to the original sale price. The borrower is sometimes said to be "doing a repo" while the lender is "doing a reverse."

A repurchase agreement can be for any term, but lots of them are just for overnight, or to cover some settlement deadline when reserve requirements have to be met.  They can be, and often are, rolled over, sometimes indefinitely (an *open repo*). From the lender's perspective, there is very little credit or liquidity risk in a repo transaction, because the collateral is good and the terms are short.  It's not a bad way to invest surplus funds, and attractive for loans substantially larger than might be appropriate for the Fed funds market.

From the borrower's perspective, it looks a little different. The loan is secured, so it's not the cheapest source of funds, even if the repo rate is typically a bit below the Fed funds rate. Also, there is a healthy amount of interest rate risk for the borrower, since the interest rate will float freely each time the loan is rolled over. On the other hand, repo transactions are available to anyone with collateral, such as money market funds, while Fed funds loans are only

---

[58]There is also *emergency credit* which is what the Fed used to bail out AIG with an $85 billion loan in 2008. Dodd-Frank curtailed the ability of the Fed to offer this kind of credit to individual companies, though it still has the power to establish an emergency credit program to aid a sector of the economy. The details of this will doubtless be worked out during the next such crisis.

available to Fed member banks. In addition to covering larger transactions, the repo market is also somewhat more private, so to speak. With the Fed funds market, everyone knows your business; with repo transactions, only the two parties really need to understand what's going on.

## More money markets for borrowing

Bank deposits, Fed funds loans, the discount window, and the repo market are all components of the world money market, but they do not make up the whole thing. There are more exotic ways for a bank to borrow funds, including currency swaps[59] and futures or issuing some kind of asset-backed security. These last typically have much longer maturities than most money market instruments, but for some reason are frequently considered to be part of the money market.

One important money market practice is the *interest rate swap*, a way banks relieve themselves from interest rate risk. Interest-rate risk is one of the important risks faced by banks, and remains on the minds of many bankers. The S&L crisis of the 1980s was largely brought about by the deregulation of interest rates in 1980. Suddenly banks could compete for customer deposits by paying higher rates, and the rates small banks were forced to pay to keep their customers rose much faster than the rates they were receiving from their long-term loans. A bank might have only been getting 6% on their 30-year loans, but suddenly found themselves having to pay that much or more in order to keep their depositors from moving their money to money-market funds, or to larger banks. This is a recipe for going out of business quickly. Small banks found themselves pursuing much more risky lending opportunities than they had had experience with, and it ended badly for many. This was a quarter-century ago, but well within the careers of many people still working in banking, both within banks as well as the bank regulators.[60]

---

[59] A *swap* is just an exchange agreement. A *credit default swap*, for example, is an agreement to exchange money for the risk that some obligation will default. A currency swap is an agreement to exchange two debts denominated in different currencies.

[60] In truth there wasn't much choice about deregulating interest rates. Inflation during the 1970s had climbed to levels much higher than the regulated interest rates, so banks were bleeding depositors desperate not to *lose* the value of their money by getting the interest they would earn by putting it in banks.

With an interest rate swap, a bank that has borrowed at a fixed rate can convert it to a floating rate by persuading someone else (paying them, cajoling them, lying to them, whatever) to assume the interest rate risk. Despite the extra risk, this may be appealing to organizations whose budgets are tightly planned years in advance, like governments whose credit isn't good enough to borrow at decent fixed rates. A bank that manages to secure a large multi-year CD, and then swap that fixed-rate debt with someone, now has a long-term, floating-rate, source of funds for which there are no reserve requirements. This is more or less a banker's holy grail.

Of course, legend has it that lots of knights perished in the search for the grail, and in this case, it's worth remembering that the only way banks can reach the grail is by finding someone else to assume risk they don't want. And there's a reason they don't want it: it's risky. This is what has happened to the Philadelphia school district. There are bankers prowling city halls and state houses all over the country looking for other people to assume interest rate risk they don't want. Philadelphia took the bait, like many others, and when interest rates plunged in the 2008 financial crisis, they all found themselves on the losing end of interest rate swaps.[61]

Again, many of the transaction possibilities are routinely available only to the biggest banks, but even a smaller bank might find ways to use the knowledge of what's possible to its benefit.

## Using the bond market

If your bank is big enough and stable enough to merit a decent bond rating, the bond market isn't a bad place to look for funds. There is a lot of money there, and a wide variety of appetites for different items on the interest rate and terms menu. This is not

---

[61]Let's look at Philadelphia's swap a bit more closely. Before the swap, Philadelphia had floating-rate debt funded by relatively fixed income (the taxes it collects). The banks, on the other hand, had fixed rate debt funded by what was very likely floating-rate income (the loans they'd made). Philadelphia feared rates going up, and increasing the cost of servicing their debt. The banks feared rates going down and decreasing their income. After the swap, Philadelphia feared rates going down. The banks, however, created a situation where they are making floating-rate debt payments with income from what are probably floating-rate loans. They no longer cared which way the rates went. Philadelphia exchanged one kind of risk for another, but the banks no longer had any at all. A nice deal for the banks, but not so nice for the students.

so very different from trolling for large CDs, but a bond is usually a longer-term investment, so will merit a bit higher interest rate. Also, the pool of buyers is far larger, so the terms can be relatively favorable to the issuing bank. Big banking institutions use the bond market extensively. The World Bank is funded almost exclusively through bonds.

An interesting player in the bond market is the Federal Home Loan Bank (FHLB), which was founded to be a conduit between the money markets and small mortgage lenders, supplying them with liquidity specifically for home finance lending. More about them on page 69.

One thing to remember is that a bond creates a liability on the bank's balance sheet, in addition to the asset of the bond proceeds. You can't add to a bank's capital via a bond, though the *owner* of a bank can do that. That is, if you own a bank, you can borrow to increase the bank's capital because it's you, not the bank, that owes it back. Your balance sheet will have matching assets to the liability for the loan you took out, but the bank you own will only see the capital.

# The banking universe

Every bank in America (the world, actually) is part of a network of other banks, each dependent on the others around it for credit, liquidity, and much more. Banks borrow from each other all the time, either in unsecured Fed funds loans, secured repo agreements, or just in deposits into accounts at their correspondent banks. Often this lending is in service of liquidity. For example, a bank running close to running out of cash on Tuesday may expect a whole bunch of customers to purchase CDs on Friday because that happens most Fridays. Those CD purchases mean the bank acquires cash, but first the bank has to get past Wednesday and Thursday, so they might borrow from a friendly bank to do that. The most likely way to deal with this is one of: an unsecured Federal funds loan (which doesn't change either bank's reserve requirement); a secured repo loan; or a secured loan from the Federal Reserve discount window (slightly longer term, but more expensive). There are other ways to address this kind of shortfall, but these are the most likely.

In other words, every bank depends on a network of other banks and financial institutions around it. Here, then, is a brief description of the important institutions, and kinds of institutions, that any bank will see as important parts of its network.

## The Federal Reserve

The Federal Reserve system is a bank-owned, public-private hybrid consisting of twelve branches around the country run by a network of boards appointed by the President.[62] All nationally-chartered banks are members, and state-chartered banks may apply to be. A member bank will keep some large fraction of its reserves on account at the Fed (with the rest in cash), and a great deal of the processing of checks and electronic payments in the country has to do with shuffling account entries among these reserve accounts. So, for example, the First National Bank of Louisiana will send a payment to the First National Bank of Montana by asking the Fed to move some money from the Louisiana reserve account to the Montana account.

In addition to this, a bank can buy Treasury securities directly from the Fed, or sell them back. It can get and redeem coins and bills in exchange for reserve account funds, and it has access the *discount window*, which we met in "Fed funds and the discount window" on page 62. The Fed is also the primary regulator of some banks, and sets accounting rules for all US banks, but those effects are sometimes a bit abstract compared to the day-to-day issues for any particular bank.

The Fed controls the *Fed funds rate*, not by setting it directly— these are transactions between one bank and another and the Fed is not a party to them, even if it holds the funds—but by managing the supply of Fed funds through *open market operations*. When the Fed wants the rate to go up, it sells Treasury bonds and collects reserve funds in exchange, often through repo agreements. This reduces the total amount of Fed funds out there and so increases the cost of borrowing those funds. When it wants to make the

---

[62]The geography of Fed branches is something of a relic of the economic state of the US in 1913. It was supposed to be dividing the country into more or less economic equivalents, but today the balance is fairly lopsided. There are, for example, two branches in the state of Missouri, and the San Francisco branch covers nine states, pretty much everything west of the Rockies. The branches are in Boston, New York City, Philadelphia, Cleveland, Richmond, Atlanta, Chicago, St. Louis, Minneapolis, Dallas, Kansas City, and San Francisco.

rate go down, it buys bonds instead. This usually works, but not always. The Fed funds rate target is usually a bit lower than the discount rate.[63]

Beyond even that, the Federal Reserve is, of course, central to the US monetary system, and there is a world of controversy surrounding it. The Fed's every move is watched by legions of commentators and analysts for what it portends for the economic future of the United States and the world. There are lots of books about the Fed and its control of the money supply. This is not one of them, though, since almost none of that is relevant to the Fed's interaction with any particular bank.

## Federal Home Loan Bank

A similar institution with very different purpose is the Federal Home Loan Bank (FHLB). Structured as a mutual bank owned by its members, the FHLB also has twelve branches around the country, though they mostly don't correspond to the Fed branch locations.[64] Membership in the FHLB is much less restrictive than the Fed, and includes banks, credit unions, thrifts, insurance companies, and community development financial institutions (CDFIs).

The point of the FHLB is to supply funds to be loaned out for long periods. Indeed, the institution was the key player in creating and promoting the concept of a long-term fixed-rate mortgage, back in the 1930s. Before that, most mortgages were five-year loans, with a balloon payment that would typically be refinanced. You can see the 30-year mortgage as a big step in democratizing finance, because it involved a huge shift in risk from the *mortgagor* (owner) to the *mortgagee* (bank). FHLB members can borrow from it for much longer terms than they can get either from the Fed or the Fed funds markets. FHLB loans (they call them *advances*) are

---

[63]Prior to the financial crisis of 2008, it was 100 basis points lower, but once the Fed funds rate hit rock bottom it wasn't possible to maintain that difference due to downward pressure on the discount rate. As of this writing, the difference is about 50 points, and will likely go back to 100 as rates rise again.

[64]These are also a relic of an earlier economic epoch, but the FHLB was chartered in 1932, a different epoch than the Fed, so its center of mass is considerably further west. The branches are in Atlanta, Boston, Chicago, Cincinatti, Dallas, Des Moines, Indianapolis, New York City, Pittsburgh, San Francisco, Seattle, and Topeka. Apparently there was a desire at the time to make sure that the FHLB cities were different from the Fed cities, but gravity will out and after a while, the original FHLB branches in Newark, NJ, Cambridge, MA, and Evanston, IL, moved to New York, Boston, and Chicago.

fully collateralized, so borrowing institutions must put up at least as much collateral as the loan amount, making the cost of funds fairly substantial. The collateral rules are quite strict, but much broader than at the Fed, though, so residential mortgages count, as do other kinds of lending. This makes FHLB into a conduit to the international financial markets for small institutions, which can make loans backed by FHLB funds.

The Bank of Sunnydale, for example, can borrow from its customers, but at least at first, it's probably too small to borrow at good rates in the bond market. The FHLB has an excellent credit rating,[65] so it can borrow at low rates in the bond market, and lend what they get to Sunnydale, along with the low rates. Sunnydale bankers can add a percent or so to the mortgage rate and lend that money out. And if they do a good job with the underwriting, they can use the resulting loans as collateral for more lending from FHLB.

## Correspondent banks

The Fed is not the only bank that other banks keep accounts with. Almost all banks have what are called *correspondent accounts* with other banks. Often this is a case of a small bank opening an account with a larger bank, usually in order to have access to some service the small bank does not offer.[66] Lots of smaller state-chartered banks are not Fed members, and those small banks can use big ones in the same way the big ones use the Fed, to hold reserves, and as a quick source of liquidity.

A bank can also join its neighbors and cooperate in lending. This will often happen when a lending opportunity arises that is just a little too big for a single bank to take on. Perhaps it's a case of avoiding concentration risk, perhaps the bank is almost tapped out, perhaps it's something else. In this case, a bank will often seek to *syndicate* a loan, sharing it with cooperating banks. (It's

---

[65]Apparently well-deserved. The FHLB came through the 2008 financial crisis with only relatively minor bruising. Of course part of their excellent rating is the implicit guarantee they enjoy from the federal government, something that was tested in the S&L crisis of the 1980s, when the FHLB was hit hard.

[66]Like money laundering, where big banks are much more efficient than little ones. In 2012, UBS, the giant Swiss bank, was found to have facilitated tax evasion for customers of Wegelin, a very small Swiss bank. There is some evidence that global drug money may have kept the international banking system afloat during 2008 and 2009. One of the lessons of the crisis might be that money laundering is a good strategy for reducing concentration risk.

also called *participation lending*.) One bank is typically the lead, and handles processing the actual loan payments, but the risk is shared. The Bank of North Dakota does a fair amount of participation lending like this, backing up North Dakota banks who want to make a loan to a valued customer, for example, but can't quite afford to do it solo.

## Banker's bank

There are banks whose purpose is to serve other banks. Sometimes characterized as a *wholesale bank*—to contrast with a *retail bank* serving customers directly—a *banker's bank* provides services that smaller banks need: liquidity management, investment advice, access to the bond market, and much more. The economies of scale mean that some services, like credit cards, lease financing, or access to the foreign currency markets are much easier to provide in the setting of a larger institution than a small community bank. Some other services, like cash management, work better as the pool of cash invested grows. And a banker's bank can be the way a smaller bank accesses the Fed's services, like the Fed funds market or buying currency, too.

A wholesale bank can also provide extra capital, chipping in when a lending opportunity is too big for a community bank, or provide a vehicle for syndicating loans among a group of banks. In a case like this, the community bank would be the lead in securing and working out the loan opportunity, but the banker's bank or other banks would supply some of the loaned funds and share in the resulting interest payments. The Bank of North Dakota is largely a wholesale operation, allowing small banks in its state to operate as if they were somewhat larger.

A related concept is a *private-label bank*. This is a bank willing to act as a bank on behalf of another organization that wants to offer banking services, but doesn't want to be a bank. When Paypal wanted to offer a debit card to its customers, they didn't become a bank, they contracted with a private-label bank willing to offer a debit card that says "Paypal" on it. The bank deals with the regulatory hassle and operates a lending operation, neither of which were important to Paypal's goal of offering a payment option to its customers.

## Investment banks

Unlike retail and commercial banks, an *investment bank* does not take deposits.[67] They have capital and find sources of funding, to be sure, but they have them in service of the underwriting and trading of securities. They underwrite bond sales, help companies acquire capital through stock sales, buy and sell the resulting securities, and about a thousand other financial services. Whereas at least some of a commercial bank's activities can be construed as making money for its depositors as well as for itself, an investment bank has no such shared goals. Certainly some of its activities are services for customers (underwriting, bond trading, dispensing financial advice), but the functions are in service to profit to the partners or shareholders.

One important function of the nation's investment banks is to be the backbone of the bond market. There is no centralized bond exchange, and bonds are traded directly from buyers to sellers, in what are called *over the counter* (*OTC*) transactions. Not all investment banks are bond dealers, and not all bond dealers are investment banks, but the two categories overlap significantly.

Investment banks are creatures of the securities industry, and as such, are regulated by the Securities and Exchange Commission (SEC) and the Financial Industry Regulatory Authority (FINRA), a non-government regulator, set up by Congress, but run by the firms it regulates.

Several of the big banks you think of when you think of big banks—Goldman Sachs, Morgan Stanley, JPMorgan Chase—are investment banks. Actually several of them are officially bank holding companies, a switch permitted during the meltdown in 2008, when Goldman Sachs, Morgan Stanley, Citigroup, and some others, were permitted to become bank holding companies in order to get access to emergency credit from the Fed.

## Investment company

An *investment company* is a very different beast from an investment bank, but they can also be useful to a bank. An investment company manages assets on behalf of a collection of partners or customers, depending on how it's incorporated. A mutual fund

---

[67]That's the official line, anyway. Investment banks often take brokered deposits. See "Managing deposits" on page 59.

is a kind of investment company, called an *open ended investment company* since it is intended to last indefinitely, with shareholders joining and leaving the pool at will. A *closed-end investment company* is basically the same thing, but with a fixed number of shares, so the only way to join is to find someone who wants to leave and buy their shares. (Some of these are traded in the stock exchanges.)

There are a few different kinds of investment companies you hear a lot about:

- A *money market fund* is an open-ended investment company that specializes in investing in highly liquid short-term securities like T-bills and commercial paper. They try to manipulate their share price to be a dollar, so that entering and exiting the fund is relatively simple. The interest a shareholder earns is awarded in more shares. They are considered to be quite secure.[68]

- A *mutual fund* is an investment company that generally implies a fairly low threshold for investors. They can invest in stocks and bonds, and there are funds out there that invest in commodities and real estate and probably in cucumber futures, too. They can be open-ended or closed-end. By being open to the general public, and with a low threshold for investors, they are subject to SEC regulations governing disclosure, insider information, and all the rest.

---

[68] Relatively speaking. The failure of Reserve Primary, a large money market fund, in the fall 2008 was probably the beginning of the real panic phase of that crisis. In the aftermath of the Lehman Brothers failure in 2008, Reserve Primary, which held a lot of Lehman paper, saw its share price drop to 97 cents. This precipitated a run on the fund and on several other funds who madly tried to sell all their commercial paper to deal with the demand for cash. The run destroyed Reserve Primary, and severely damaged the others. Lots of big corporations use commercial paper to finance purchases of parts and materials, and they were suddenly cut off, unable to sell notes at all. They couldn't turn to banks because lots of them rely on the short-term market for liquidity, and suddenly it wasn't liquid. The resulting plunge in the short-term bond market was the real source of panic among bank regulators that fall, when they realized the Lehman failure would become much more than simply teaching errant bankers the sins of their ways, and that it would have real repercussions on the real economy. Lehman closed on September 15, a Monday, Reserve Primary dropped on Tuesday, other funds were hammered on Wednesday. On Friday morning, chastened Treasury Department officials announced it would guarantee deposits in money market funds.

- A *hedge fund* is (usually) a closed-end investment company that invests however it pleases. These funds are open only to *accredited investors*, the SEC's term for "rich and supposedly sophisticated investors." The idea is that only savvy investors should be let into this jungle, and so they wash their hands of regulating the jungle. Hedge fund fees tend to be high, the industry standard is what they call "2-and-20." They charge an annual management fee of 2% of assets under management and take 20% of the investment gains—though not the losses.[69]

- A *private equity fund* is an investment company, also usually closed-end and exempt from many SEC rules regarding investment companies. A private equity fund's purpose is to make equity investments in existing companies. There's a lot to say about the private equity industry, but in a book about banks, it will suffice to say that private equity companies have been the primary device through which industry in the US has been financialized over the past 40 years. That is, through the private equity industry, financial managers without a deep connection to the business of some company have supplanted the people who came to management through years of experience in that particular business. The value supplied by the new managers remains controversial, to say the least. Private equity funds also typically use the 2-and-20 formulation for fees.

- A special-purpose private equity fund, designed to help startup businesses with their capital investment, is called a *venture capital fund*.

---

[69]The fee structure and the unregulated nature of these funds is partly why you hear so much about hedge fund and private equity managers who have become incredibly wealthy through their hedge funds. Curiously, one has a much harder time finding hedge fund *customers* who have become incredibly wealthy through their hedge fund activities. One would cry few tears for these supposedly savvy investors being so exploited, except that many of them are actually our municipal comptrollers, pension fund managers, or county treasurers.

# Payments

When you get right down to it, money is a pretty ethereal concept. It's possible to talk forever about what it actually is without coming to a conclusion. However ethereal money itself is, the representation of money is pretty straightforward. It might be pieces of paper or metal, and it might be electrons or some molecules of iron oxide on the back of a bank card. Whatever it is, a system that moves money or a representation of money from one person to another (or one bank to another, as the case may be) is a *payment system*. Since it all connects together, some people will say the world has just one payment system, but calling the whole big crazy quilt a single "system" seems kind of a stretch.

A payment system is not only the technology, but the rules and procedures that make it work, and make it secure. C.E. Beckman Co., a 100-year-old ship's chandlery in New Bedford, MA, had an interesting payment system. Clerks would write up your order on a slip and tuck the slip into a pneumatic tube that would take it down the block to the cashier's office. You'd then have to follow it there to pay for your order, and the cashier would use another pneumatic tube to send back permission for you to pick up the order. The result was they could keep the cash in a single secured room and didn't have to walk it down the street at closing in what was a pretty tough dockfront neighborhood. They could also hire clerks they couldn't trust with money, something else important in a neighborhood where sailors needed work for a few months when they were on shore, but then would ship out for a year or more at a time.

Beckman's payment system consisted of the pneumatic tubes, the cashier's office, and the rules and procedures people used to operate it. It was designed to be secure against the risks they faced. Other payment systems are designed with similar concerns to protect against different risks. This is why your debit card requires a PIN number and your checks require a signature.

There is, as you might imagine, an endless variety of payment systems beyond the simple exchange of cash. This section describes some of the more important systems in the US.

# Checks

A *check* is a familiar payment system to most people. It is the most common form of what's called a *draft*, an order from you that your bank pay another party. Some checks are presented at the bank that issued them and exchanged for cash, but most are deposited in some other bank.

When one bank winds up with a check written on another bank, it has to arrange for the check to be returned to the issuing bank, in exchange for money. This is *check clearing*. Many banks have arrangements with correspondent banks to return checks directly, while a check written on some distant bank has to be submitted to a *clearing house*. Transferring money incurs charges, so a bank doesn't want to make a transfer for every single check. The clearing house accumulates all the checks issued over some period, usually a day, and consolidates the transactions they represent.[70] If at the end of the day, Bank A has $5,000 in checks from Bank B, who has $4,000 checks from Bank A, the transfers cancel out a little and result in only a single transfer of $1,000 from Bank B to Bank A.

Once the transactions are consolidated, the clearing house still has to make the transfers happen, and that involves creating instructions for them and issuing them to some settlement bank where each of the banks involved has an account. The Fed operates the largest clearing house, and also operates the National Settlement Service (NSS) that executes a whole set of account transfers at once, for its clearing house, and others. Of course, it can only provide that service for banks that have an account at the Fed.

Check payment has several security features, ranging from the signature on the check itself to the lists of bad-check passers stuck in a folder next to the grocery store cash register. One important security feature, widely used by big companies or governments is called *positive pay*. With positive pay, the company sends the bank a list of the checks it has written and the bank agrees to honor only checks on that list. This allows an account's checks to be under the control of several different offices within that business or government.

---

[70]Obviously a clearing house can only clear checks from banks it knows about. Other checks have to be forwarded to another clearing house that might have better luck with them.

Some banks offer an elaboration of the check payment system, a *lockbox service*, which is an address, with a bunch of people there to open envelopes containing bill payments and deposit what's inside. This can be a more secure option for many offices, and makes the funds available much more quickly. Some lockbox services will offer the ability to print and mail the bills, too. There are also courier companies doing roughly the same thing by planting an actual lockbox—a steel box with a lock on it—on your premises and emptying it on some regular schedule.[71]

## Electronic payments

Electronic payments are quickly growing in importance. There are well over 80 billion such transactions in the US each year, with a value of over $50 trillion. By the time you read this, the numbers will be greater since they appear to be growing each year at an annual rate of about 5%. Electronic payments are supplanting both payments by check and payment by cash.

There are two important variants of electronic payments: instant and netting. An instant system, also called a *real-time gross settlement* transfer (*RTGS*) makes the transaction happen right away. A *wire transfer* is an RTGS transaction. In the US, the *Fedwire* system, operated by the Fed, carries the bulk of these transactions, which produce a transfer from one account at the Fed to another. There is a substantial charge for these transactions, so they are typically only used for large transfers of funds.

An example of a netting system with a much smaller membership is the Clearing House Interbank Payment System (CHIPS). CHIPS has a bit less than 50 members, as opposed to the 9,000 or so Fed members. However, its members are quite large, and most of them are not based in the US, so it makes a very good route for large international transfers of money. CHIPS members pre-fund a fraction of their anticipated transactions for a day as security, and then make up the balances at the end of the day. CHIPS is a *netting engine*, that accumulates a day's transactions, composes them into a set of final payments, and settles them all at once.

---

[71]For those who enjoy debating what money really is, consider that some of these companies will credit your account for money you've put into the box *before* they send their armored truck out to get it. A business or government using this service can spend money while it is still locked inside a small steel box in their offices. If you can spend the money, then what, exactly, is in the box?

For smaller transactions, the most important system (in the US) is called *ACH* which stands for *automated clearing house*. ACH transactions include things like direct-deposit of payroll and government benefits, direct bill-pay from consumer bank accounts, and direct-pay business-to-business payments. It's not a bad approximation to think of ACH as just an electronic check. In the same way that a bank forwards its checks to a clearing house, a bank will transmit ACH payment requests to an ACH operator, who accumulates those payments into a set of consolidated payments over some time, like a day. There are several different ACH operators out there, though again the Fed operates the biggest by far, handling billions of transactions every year.

## Credit and debit cards

Bank cards have, in the past forty years, gone from being a novelty to an integral part of the flow of funds in the economy. They have proliferated in variety, too, but come in two main varieties: credit cards and debit cards.

You can think of a credit card as representing two different payments, from the bank to the merchant and from you to the bank. When you buy a doughnut with a credit card, the baker swipes your card through their machine, which notifies their bank (the *acquiring bank*) that you're hungry for a doughnut. They check with your bank, who authorizes the transaction, and so the baker releases the doughnut and you eat it. (Some merchants might skip this authorization step, for a variety of different reasons having to do with the size of the transaction and the relationship between the merchant and the bank.)

Later that day, the baker collects all the credit card slips collected during the day and submits them in a batch to their bank, who sends them along to the *credit card association*. This is the governing body for that brand of card: Visa, MasterCard, Discover, and the rest. The association clears the transactions, sorting and consolidating them into payment instructions and debiting the account of your *issuing bank* (the one who issued the card to you) and crediting the merchant's bank, who then pays the merchant. It's now the issuing bank's problem to get the money from you, and they send a bill. Money flows from your bank to the association to the baker's bank to the baker, and then from you to your issuing bank when you pay the bill. The issuing bank may not be the bank where you have a checking account, so there is a bank transfer involved there, too.

As you can imagine, there is a certain amount of settling and consolidation done throughout the process. The merchant accumumlates a day's worth of credit card receipts before submitting them to their bank. The credit-card association settles transactions among all the customer and merchant banks they deal with, and the customer's payment is settled through the usual check-clearing process. There is quite a lot of money in the pipeline at any time.

There is a certain amount of credit risk a bank takes on when it issues credit cards. Most credit card debt is unsecured, and there is a bit of a mismatch between the date the debt is incurred and the date interest begins to accrue. For example, if you paid for that doughnut on the first day of the billing month, the merchant will get their money for it a couple of days later, but it's still almost a month before the bank issues the bill and another few weeks before you pay it. The bank is earning no interest unless you put off paying the bill and start to accumulate a balance. Despite this, banks have found credit cards to be quite a profitable business, partly through fee income (from both the consumer and merchant) and partly because in 1978, the Supreme Court ruled that state-by-state usury limits (interest rate limits) only applied to the banks within those states, not to the customers. Issuing banks proceeded to move *en masse* to Delaware, Nevada, and South Dakota, where there are no interest rate limits, and have lived happily ever after, charging interest rates that would have made Pierpont Morgan himself blanch.

A *debit card* is quite a bit simpler than a credit card, because the money flows directly from the bank account associated with the card to the merchant's bank account. Like credit cards, debit card transactions also undergo a settling and clearing process, to minimize the number of transactions the banks have to pay for. (The process differs, depending on whether you signed for the debit transaction, or entered a PIN into a POS terminal.) Some lag is thus built into all these systems, time to let the transactions accumulate with the goal being to economize on the cost of the actual transactions.

There are also pre-pay debit cards now, where instead of the card being an accessory to the account, it represents the account. A customer pays some money and gets a card that "contains" the money, which can be spent the same way another debit card is used, at an ATM, or a store. Because these can be dispensed and refilled at stores, like cell phone minutes, these have become an important source of banking services to poor people who might not have any other bank.[72]

The ATM network is an important component of the card payment systems. When you withdraw cash from an ATM, or from the *point-of-sale terminal* (*POS*) at a grocery store, the ATM network signals approval from your bank, and then you withdraw cash from the ATM owner's cash account while an ACH transaction to match it is created. You get the cash immediately, but it takes a day or so for the corresponding ACH transaction to clear.

ATM transactions are one of the few payment systems that involve the actual movement of physical money. The movement is not a result of the transaction itself, but of the truck that brought cash to put into the ATM in the first place. The customer then takes the money and moves it further.

## Securities

Among the interesting payment systems out there are payment systems for securities. When you buy a government bond, it is very seldom that you actually receive a piece of paper in exchange. The vast bulk of US Government bonds exist only as entries in the Fed's electronic ledger.[73] When a bond is bought or sold, the entries in the ledger change to record the new ownership. There is a whole welter of rules and procedures to make sure that it happens properly and only after payment has been verified. Of course since the payment probably consists of transfers between Fed members, this is generally not difficult.

A very similar kind of arrangement works for municipal bonds, commercial paper, and a large number of the stocks for sale on US exchanges. Almost all of these are kept at the Depository Trust & Clearing Corporation (DTCC). Buyers and sellers ex-

---

[72]And an important avenue to exploit those poor people, too. Companies that demand their employees be paid via direct deposit have increasingly turned to prepay debit cards for employees without a bank account. But many such cards have significant fees for withdrawals, so cashing a paycheck might cost a few dollars, a big deal to a minimum-wage worker.

[73]A notable exception is the Social Security Administration, which—by order of Congress—keeps the bonds that make up the Social Security Trust Fund in a locked file cabinet at the Bureau of the Public Debt in Parkersburg, West Virginia.

change entries in the DTCC database. Until the DTC (the DTCC's predecessor) was founded in 1973, brokers would exchange real pieces of paper when a security was sold. The messenger business in Manhattan was a growth industry in the 1960s, when the volume of securities traded escalated dramatically. Between 1965 and 1968, volume on the New York Stock Exchange tripled, and it became ever more difficult to keep up with the paperwork. The advent of the DTC relieved the market participants from the burden, and increased security besides.

## Mobility

What's amusing about these payment systems is how similar they are to Victorian England. From the middle of the 19th century until the 1920s, London was the financial capital of the world. Almost all the world's gold was stored in vaults at the Bank of England and a small number of banks in its orbit. This gold was stored on behalf of businesses and governments around the world. International trade was made possible by cross-border capital flows that often consisted of a clerk in London scratching out one accounting ledger entry and making another. One hundred years later, money moves in much the same fashion, by changing ledger entries at a single location.

As ethereal as money is, it takes physical arrangements like these payment systems to move it around. What's more, in many of these systems, the money is stationary and what moves is the directions to move money from one account to another in a single bank. A check you write could cross the country once to make some payment, and then back again to be cleared, with the result being a couple of ledger lines changed at the Federal Reserve. You want to send money to India? Your local credit union might make a deposit at BankAmerica with a check drawn on its correspondent bank, which would result in transferring money from one account to another at the Fed. Funds "at" BankAmerica, but actually on account at the Fed, could then be transferred via CHIPS to the State Bank of India by transferring money between accounts at the Bank for International Settlements (BIS) the central bank for central banks, located in Basel, Switzerland. The State Bank of India would then transfer the funds to one of its member banks, until it reaches an account owned by your recipient.

## New forms of payments

Ironically, though capital is as mobile today as it has been in history, it is still the physical manifestations of money that travel much farther and more often than the insubstantial forms. Cash—paper and metal—travels in people's pockets and in armored trucks that supply a bank's branches and ATMs. The ethereal and abstract forms of money—accounts at the Fed or the DTC, for example—tend to be immobile, even if they can be traded all over the world. Orders to pay may travel by mail and over wires, but the funds themselves don't.

This is the innovation of *bitcoin*, and what makes it so different from any other form of electronic funds. A bitcoin uses sophisticated encryption to create a pattern of bits whose origin and history can be verified by decoding it. A central registry records the date and time of transactions, which are also recorded in the bitcoin itself. Once a bitcoin changes hands, the bits representing the coin itself also change, and any pre-change copies become obvious fakes. The history of dates in the registry must match the dates recorded in the bitcoin, but the registry does not record who owns the bitcoin. It is thus an anonymous form of payment, and can be sent in an email or uploaded to a distant web site, exactly what has made it popular among drug smugglers and gamblers.

Another related innovation is in the use of cell phone minutes. In parts of Africa, informal markets have developed with brokers able to sell minutes to pre-pay cell phone plans. When brokers appeared who were also willing to buy them, it became possible to send money across borders by sending the codes to unlock cell phone minutes. You can buy minutes in one country and text the code numbers to unlock the minutes to someone in another country, who can sell that code for cash.

More formal cell phone payment systems are coming online, too. They are already widely used in many countries. When you pay for something with a cell phone, you have more or less initiated a debit card transaction, but with the amount paid to appear on your phone bill instead of being debited from your bank account. The phone company, in turn, has a settlement account at some Fed member bank, and uses that to send or receive the payment from the other party.

There seem to be few limits to the variety of payment systems out there, and fewer still for the variety yet to be invented. It's not clear where bitcoin itself is going, for example, but the technology has been invented and is there for someone else to use if they can figure out how. In the same way, innovations in card technology and cell phone payments will change the way we use money, and the way we think of it.

# Where are the magic beans?

> The other day in a banker's care,
> I saw some money that wasn't there.
> It wasn't there again today,
> I wish I wish it would go away.
>
> *Not by Hughes Mearns (1875–1965).*

So after all this, where's the magic part, where banks create money?

In one sense the magic of money creation is, like all stage magic, an illusion that depends on where you're standing. The banker doesn't see money being created. The banker sees him or herself taking a risk by loaning out some money that's been deposited, and managing that risk somehow. Ask a banker where the money creation happens, and he or she might give you a funny look.

From outside the bank, though, it looks different. An observer of some bank might see customers deposit a million dollars into it, and then watch while its loan officers make $900,000 in loans out of that, keeping 10% for reserves. (Presumably this bank has some capital as well.) This is where the money is created, because the depositors still assume they have $1 million in the bank,[74] and

---

[74] A friend and I joked once that this was like the quantum mechanics of money. When a bank creates a loan, they typically just open a checking account for the borrower and say there is money in it. (See page 50.) Just like a subatomic particle that could be here and could be there, it could be said that the money is now in two places at once: in the borrower's account, but also in the accounts of the original depositors. This is one of those analogies that has more truth in it than the analogy-makers originally recognized, for while the usual interpretation of quantum mechanics does allow for a wave function to imply that a particle is in two places at once, this is only true until you actually measure the particle's location.

the borrowers are free to take their $900,000 wherever they want, and now the economy has $1.9 million where before it had only one million. This is the *multiplier*, and it can be applied again by whatever bank receives the loaned money.

Unless the loaned money is kept on account at the lending bank, it isn't available to that bank any more. If the loaned money was withdrawn, the bank that loaned out $900,000 now only has $100,000 of the original million sitting around (plus the agreements with its borrowers) to manage its depositors' needs. The managers hope they made the right choices of borrowers, but managing those choices is all they can do. A single bank can't do any more than apply the multiplier once to its deposits, though a banking *system* can apply it indefinitely.[75]

Huge banks, or banks with a dominant position in some local market, can count on a fair amount of funds being returned to them. BankAmerica, for example, will see a relatively large number of the recipients of their loans doing their banking at BankAmerica. Because they have so many customers, lots of the money they loan will make its way back into some BankAmerica account. A smaller bank, or a public bank with a relatively small number of customers, can't count on that. Those banks can participate in the multiplier, but they cannot own the results without the deposits returning to them.

All is not lost, though. Even a smaller bank that loans out some money might be able to count on the money taking some time to exit the bank. Say the $900,000 loan above was in service of some construction project estimated to take two years. If the customer shares the draw-down plan with the bank—as would be typical

---

At that point, you know that it's only in one place.

In precisely the same way, you can imagine the money being in two different accounts at the same time—and some people do make a big thing out of this—but this illusion vanishes the moment the money's location is measured. What's the analogy for "measuring" money here? Withdrawing it. At some point, the depositor will return for his or her money, or the borrower will write a check and some other bank will return the check to the original bank. At that moment, the money's location is known, and the bank has to be able to produce it in some form the customer or other bank will approve. None of these are unusual events, so this analogy is really only for amusement value, and that's why it's in a footnote and not in the text.

[75]Lots of the loaned funds will leak out of the banking system and become either currency instead or deposits that move too fast to lend (bankers might call them too "hot" to lend), so the multiplier only reaches its mathematical maximum under unusual circumstances.

of a public construction project like building a bridge or a sewage treatment plant—the bank can continue to count on some of that money to be on deposit, and can use it accordingly, perhaps for a short-term loan or investment.

As we saw in "Borrowing" on page 58, another way the original bank can get more funds to loan is borrow them from other banks, and the multiplier can work on this money, too. For example, the original bank here might seek to borrow $900,000 from other banks to make up for its loans. This kind of borrowing, in the Fed funds market, is common, but the unsecured loans are generally for very short terms, often overnight. These can usually be rolled over ad infinitum, but a bank incurs a fair amount of interest rate risk doing so, since the rate they pay will be quite volatile, depending heavily on the the borrowing bank's credit rating, the broader financial markets, and the weather. A bank wouldn't want to make long term fixed rate loans with this money, except maybe with the cooperation of the other bank, and even then, only warily. Slightly longer-term money is available in the repo market, but those are secured loans, so the cost of the funds is higher than the interest rate would have you believe. Most banks will have better luck with something like the FHLB's secured advances to expand their lending.

In other words, while the multiplier can in theory be applied indefinitely, real-world considerations—such as a clear-eyed assessment of the risks a bank is incurring—will often prevent it from reaching its theoretical maximum. Of course, lots of bankers do not have such clear eyes.

In the sample balance sheets on page 31, you can see the degree to which the different banks rely on borrowing from parties other than their depositors. BankAmerica has $67 billion outstanding in other borrowing and $61 billion in the Fed funds market, compared to deposits of $1.2 trillion. This is about 5-10%, and probably consistent with using that money mainly for liquidity management. Washington Trust, on the other hand, has $417 million borrowed and $2.2 billion in deposits. This is 19%, and consistent with the suspicion that Washington Trust is much closer to its lending limit than either of the larger banks, BankAmerica or RBS Citizens.

## Four

## Bank regulation

ONE UNAVOIDABLE LESSON of the 2008 banking crisis is that government regulation of banks is an essential part of maintaining a decent banking system. For those with a philosophical bent, you could say the push of banks creates innovation and activity and the pull of the regulators creates safety and security. Actual events have only vaguely approximated that ideal, so those with a more jaundiced view of the world might say something else entirely.

As the foundations of the financial system crumbled in the fall of 2008, Alan Greenspan, president of the Federal Reserve from 1987 to 2006, spoke about self-regulation in testimony to Congress:

> "[T]hose of us who have looked to the self-interest of lending institutions to protect shareholders equity (myself especially) are in a state of shocked disbelief."

Much of bank regulation is the oversight designed to keep banks solvent through monitoring of the balance sheet and the regulatory ratios outlined in the beginning of this book. There are, however, issues that go beyond these, not least the changing landscape of banking.

As with the rest of this book, this chapter can hardly be considered to cover the vast number of questions and answers surrounding bank regulation. It is, instead, an introduction to the players, and a discussion of some important points that will help you learn further from more exhaustive sources.

# Who are the regulators?

The US operates the world's most fractured bank regulation system. Historically speaking, it grew and changed with the exigencies of different eras, and lives on largely due to the success—so far—of US banks, but really, no one would design from scratch a regulatory system with such a proliferation of bank regulators.

There are two categories of regulators: state and federal. Each state has its own bank regulator, and the federal government has four more. State-chartered banks are regulated by their home states. National banks are regulated by the Office of the Comptroller of the Currency (OCC), part of the Treasury Department. The Federal Reserve also regulates state-chartered banks that are Fed members, and the FDIC regulates the ones that are not, though it insures all of them. There's also the National Credit Union Administration (NCUA), which both regulates and insures credit unions.

The various regulators do not use remarkably different approaches to regulation. They all use the same regulatory ratios and have much the same goals. However, regulators are granted a great deal of discretion to interpret the ratios and the other measures, and this creates a difference in result. In the past, the regulators have enjoyed fairly different reputations for toughness—the late Office of Thrift Supervision (OTS) was known for its laxness, for example. Among the scandals of the US banking system is that banks can, and do, "shop" for their regulators by changing their charters.[76] The agency reputations are somewhat in flux, if only because in the aftermath of the biggest banking disaster in 70 years, there are no sure things. And OTS was closed and merged with OCC, so someone else has to become the lax one.

In addition to these, the Bank for International Settlements (BIS), in Switzerland, plays a part in coordinating international

---

[76]In 2007, when Countrywide Financial found itself under pressure from the OCC about its deteriorating financial condition, they changed their charter from a national bank to a savings bank, thereby coming under the "scrutiny" of the OTS, known as a more lenient regulator. Bank regulators assess fees from the banks they regulate and astonishingly, OTS actually lobbied Countrywide to make the change, in order to increase its fee revenue. In other words, not only can banks choose their regulator, but US regulators sometimes compete to attract banks. OTS-regulated banks, including Countrywide, IndyMac, and Washington Mutual, constituted their own shameful parade of disaster and insolvency, largely why the office was abolished by the Dodd-Frank legislation and its functions transferred to OCC.

banking accords, like the Basel agreements. In theory, these are supposed to be agreements to harmonize banking regulations across borders, since so many banks operate internationally these days. In practice, the international regulations are sometimes used as clubs with which to subdue national banking regulators who might prefer a stricter approach to regulation than international banks like.

These are not the only regulators out there. The big mortgage insurance agencies (FHA, VA) exert considerable influence on the banking industry by specifying what kinds of mortgages they will insure, and the Financial Accounting Standards Board (FASB) and the Governmental Accounting Standards Board (GASB) are private organizations of accountants, who set accounting standards (also known as generally accepted accounting principles, or GAAP) for public companies and governments in the US, respectively. FASB gets its authority from the SEC, and GASB gets its authority largely from precedent and widespread use.

## Other players

There are other important regulatory players in the financial markets.

- The Securities and Exchange Commission (SEC) regulates investment companies and investment banks. It was created in 1934 to ride herd on the stock market, and now has a portfolio of regulatory responsibility as long as your arm. The rule of thumb is that if it is financial, and not strictly banking, the SEC is probably the regulator—if anyone is.

- The Financial Industry Regulatory Authority (FINRA) is an independent, non-governmental financial industry regulator. It was formed in 2007, spun off by combining the regulatory and enforcement divisions of the New York Stock Exchange (NYSE) and the National Association of Securities Dealers (NASD). These were the offices in those exchanges that set and enforced standards for the stocks traded on the NYSE and on NASDAQ, the electronic exchange. Although the SEC approved the creation of FINRA, it is not part of the government. Its budget comes from the fees it assesses its members, and the members staff its Board of Governors, along with some public members. FINRA is supposed to oversee brokers and dealers, and the SEC is supposed to oversee FINRA. With only a few years of a track record, it's hard to say how effective a regulator it is. However, one can say that a stock exchange's interests are not always aligned with those of its member brokers, so a regulator run by the stock exchange would have incentive to be tough with brokers. FINRA is now run by the very companies it regulates, so it is not at all clear how tough it can or will be.

- The Municipal Securities Rulemaking Board (MSRB) sets rules for municipal bonds and the brokers and dealers in such things. Created by Congress in 1975, it is, like FINRA, organized as a self-regulator, and it is controlled by a board of municipal bond brokers and dealers. However, apart from the mixed bag of its service as a regulator, the MSRB runs the invaluable emma.msrb.org, where you can find bond prices, yields, and trading history.

- The Commodity Futures Trading Commission (CFTC) is the government body in charge of futures and options markets in the US. Most of the activity in those markets has little to do with banks, strictly.[77] Unfortunately, the derivatives that *do* have to do with banks, like interest-rate swaps and credit-default swaps, remain largely unregulated, and traded not on an exchange, but *over the counter* (*OTC*), financial industry slang for securities sold from one party to another in private deals, rather than through an *exchange* with a trading floor and (more importantly) standards for the products traded.[78]

- The FFIEC is the Federal Financial Institutions Examination Council. It is not really a regulator, but more sort of an inter-agency bureau whose mission is to ameliorate, to the extent

---

[77]Though the big investment banks, like Goldman Sachs and JPMorgan, have invested heavily in the commodities markets, driving up the price of food, oil, aluminum, and more with their speculation. This is a number 10 size can of worms best left to sort out in another book.

[78] Brooksley Born, the CFTC director from 1996 to 1999, has become justly famous for trying (and failing) to bring OTC derivatives under regulatory control before they became a disaster. Unfortunately for all of us, she was thwarted by free-marketeers in the Clinton administration and Congress who were certain that banks would be too concerned about (a) their reputations or (b) their solvency to abuse these, um, important financial innovations. In the event, concern about these did not turn out to be an effective control, once again to Alan Greenspan's "state of shocked disbelief" (*SOSD*).

it can, the crazily fractured nature of bank regulation in the US. It tries to standardize report forms and definitions, for example, and tries, with mixed success, to promote a uniform approach to regulation. For people who don't work at one of those agencies, it is most notable for being the repository for quarterly financial reports from all banks, bank holding companies, and credit unions, no matter which regulator. These reports, officially called *Consolidated Report on Condition and Income*, are commonly called a bank's *call report*.[79] The FFIEC condenses the call reports into *Uniform Bank Performance Reports*, calculating a bunch of regulatory ratios for you. They issue a similar report for bank holding companies. They have a better-than-decent web site for looking up a bank's *UBPR* or its *UBHPR* if it's actually a bank holding company: ffiec.gov.

In addition to all these, the Dodd-Frank legislation of 2011 created the Consumer Financial Protection Bureau (CFPB), an agency housed in the Federal Reserve, whose purpose is to regulate financial products marketed to consumers. Though founded in 2011, the agency did not have a director named until the Senate overcame two years of filibuster to confirm Richard Cordray in July of 2013. Consequently, it's a little soon to tell anything at all about the agency, except that it has its work cut out for it.

## Community Reinvestment Act

The Community Reinvestment Act (CRA). The CRA was passed in 1977 to combat the practice of *redlining*, or excluding certain neighborhoods from a bank's business. Through the 1960s and 1970s, as urban flight became epidemic, large swaths of our nation's cities found themselves with no bank branches at all. The CRA was passed to say that banks have a responsibility to serve *all* of our community, both the poor neighborhoods, and the better-off ones. Essentially it adds a set of social-responsibility criteria to

---

[79]There was a day when quarterly reports were collected for dates chosen as a surprise—"called"—by the federal bank regulators. The idea was to prevent banks from manipulating their books to make things look better on a particular day than on the day before or after. (Lehman Brothers successfully used repo transactions this way, right up until its bitter end.) This practice of surprise reporting was ended in the 1960s, a decision not without controversy at the time.

the usual solvency questions a bank examination is supposed to consider.

The CRA does not demand banks operate at a loss, but it does require them to show they do not ignore any neighborhoods within their service area. Furthermore, the CRA gives community groups the right to comment on banks' compliance with the act, and it requires regulators to take those comments into account when considering bank mergers or expansion plans. CRA examinations are not done very often (the FFIEC web site does a good job of collating CRA reports from the various regulators) and the ratings awarded can follow a bank for years. Consequently, the act gives activists an important tool to pressure banks into paying attention to the communities in which they live.

There remains considerable controversy about how banks demonstrate their commitment to a neighborhood during a CRA examination. The CRA does not require banks to write bad loans, and the percentage of credit-worthy customers in a poor neighborhood is likely to be lower than in a wealthier area, so simple comparisons of loan concentration will not be appropriate measures. The OTS used to have a formula that 50% of the CRA rating be lending activity, 25% be consumer services such as deposits and branch presence, and 25% be investments, but the OTS has expired, as has that rule. The other regulators use different rules, and the act itself is under constant discussion and revision in Congress.

# Federal Deposit Insurance Corporation

The FDIC is such an integral part of bank operation in the US that most bank customers won't even need to have its name spelled out. The Federal Deposit Insurance Corporation is another legacy of the bank disasters of the Great Depression. Before that, there was no insurance for bank deposits, and a depositor had to keep a wary eye on their bank's health in order to keep their money safe. And routinely, this wasn't enough. Local bank panics were common throughout the country, and there were widespread financial panics in the US that brought down hundreds of banks, in 1819, 1837, 1857, 1873, 1893, 1907. And then it got worse. The 1920s saw an average of more than five hundred banks a year closing their doors. In 1933 alone, 4,000 banks failed. Most of these failures left the bulk of their depositors high and dry. The devastation to individuals was bad enough, but the failure of a bank of any significant size had a huge impact on local economies.

Worse than that, sometimes a perfectly healthy bank could fail, done in by little more than rumor. No bank keeps all its deposits hanging around in cash, so a bank run can doom even the best-run institution. Rough experience showed that a run could begin for little or no reason, though obviously some runs were on institutions that richly deserved one. In the free-for-all climate that existed, a bank's reputation was crucial, and there was very little protection beyond that. The necessity for constant bolstering of that reputation is partly why bank notes, stock certificates and insurance policies of the day were elaborately printed, in multiple colors, often on gilt-edged paper. It wasn't just protection against counterfeit, it was also an advertisement that the company could afford such luxury, and therefore was secure enough to take care of your money.

The Banking Act of 1933 changed all that by creating the FDIC to insure depositors' money. Now, while banks obviously still fail, depositors are not at risk, at least up to the $250,000 insurance limit.[80] Banks pay the FDIC an insurance premium (called an *assessment* in their jargon) based on the size of their deposits, usually in the range of 5–35 cents per hundred dollars of deposits. The FDIC assessments depend on the bank's size and the risk category into which FDIC examiners classify a bank.

In the event of a bank failure, the FDIC also acts as the receiver, and does the work of unwinding the bank's liabilities and paying whatever can be paid to whom, or looking for a buyer if the remaining carcass still has some value. Shareholders in the bank are usually wiped out, as are the bondholders, though they have a superior claim in case anything is left after selling the assets.

---

[80] Above that limit, depositors are just another creditor, though with priority over bondholders, who have priority over shareholders. Some large depositors, such as most governments, demand collateral as security for their deposits. The collateral is supposed to be assigned to a third party (often the FHLB) so there is some security there. Of course when a giant falls, there is a big mess, and unusual things can happen. Derivative contracts, for example, are also collateralized, at least in theory, and with some large banks party to derivative transactions in the trillions of dollars, there is no telling what effect that might have on other creditors. In other words, no one should contemplate a large bank failure with complacency, no matter what legal agreements bind their deposits.

The FDIC does not provide deposit insurance for credit unions, but the NCUA, an almost perfectly parallel organization designed for them, does.

# Evaluating and modeling risk

Risk-weighting a bank's assets is not the only way to assess the risk inherent in its portfolio. More recently, banks have come to rely on a concept called *value at risk*, or *VaR*. This is a dollar measure of how much value a bank is likely to lose in a given time period, assuming conditions go bad. If the VaR for some bank is $80 million at 95% confidence for a day, this means that if tomorrow is a *very* bad day, the probability is 95% that the bank's losses on the value of its portfolio will be no more than $80 million. This can be made to be a more precise number than the risk-weighted assets, and so has been more attractive to a certain species of bank management.

The VaR is a convenient, at-a-glance, measurement of risk, but calculating it is fraught with a number of assumptions. You calculate it through *risk modeling* which sounds very high-tech, but is pretty simple at root. (And pretty simple to game.) The idea is that you look at the fluctuation of asset prices over some period of time where market conditions are roughly like they are now. Any asset in a bank's portfolio—bonds, mortgages, real estate, whatever—will record some variation in price. Most days, the variation will be minor, and some days it will be large. You set some threshold, say 95%, and exclude the 5% of the variations that are the largest. Now take the largest dip in prices remaining, and apply that to the assets that are actually in your bank's portfolio. Add up the losses, and that's your VaR. The math behind all this is the risk model.

That's the basic idea, but there are endless variations. You might choose a different probability threshold or a different time period to analyze. Some asset prices are *inversely correlated*, that is, they tend to move in opposite directions on any particular day. Stocks and bonds usually act this way; a good day on the stock market is usually a bad day for a bond investor. Risk modelers might assume that when one class of assets drops in price, the other class will appreciate. If you build that into your model of a bank that has some of both, you could predict that a very bad day might not seem quite as bad. Beyond that, you might come up with a more sophisticated way to identify the period of history that is most "like" the period we're in now, or realize that you'd forgotten to account for the effect of investor expectations, which might dampen a steep drop or rise in prices. These are, of course, just assumptions, not really so far from astrology, but if you can gussy them up in enough math, few will notice. Of the few people who actually took a statistics class in school, half of them were sleeping.

And that's the big problem with risk modeling and thus with VaR itself. The process is lousy with assumptions, not just in how the models are constructed, but in the data that go into it. Why 95%? Why this period of history? Why assume the future is statistically like the past? Once you get into the weeds of any specific model, you find even more assumptions, some of them backed up by little more than plausible hunches. Modeling is a valuable tool, and you can learn a lot from using a good one, but it is very easy to abuse. For a statistician with good enough rhetorical skills, a good suit, and a command of terms like heteroskedasticity,[81] a wide range of modeling assumptions can be justified to people who have a weaker command of statistics. If one set of assumptions makes those statistical innocents happier than another, and thus more likely to award the statistician a bonus, well, perhaps you can see where this is going.

The other big problem with risk modeling stares you in the face, but lots of people don't see it because they don't bother to do the math. That is, if there is a 95% chance of something not happening tomorrow, that sounds like a pretty sure bet. But this is the same as a 5% chance of that something happening after all. If you make that bet on twenty consecutive days, you will almost certainly lose once, since $20 \times 5\% = 100\%$. A 99% sure thing will fail one day out of a hundred, and something that happens on 99.9% of days will fail once or twice every three years, guaranteed.

Unfortunately, VaR is trendy now. People who understand the role modeling played in underestimating the risk of mortgage bonds before the 2008 crisis are wary, but the method is still in

---

[81]This just means a measurement that varies more in one subgroup than another. A measurement of the heights of an entire population would be heteroskedastic because among children height varies much more than among adults.

wide use. The appearance of precision is attractive, as is the ability
to tailor the model to the hunches and experience of the bankers
who use them. Many banks and investment banks use these models to assess risk in their trading accounts, and the SEC and bank
regulators rely on the results of these models to say how much
risk a bank has in its trading account. The regulators have developed some techniques for assessing the risk models themselves,
but for a sufficiently complicated model, this is an uphill battle. In
other words, regulators have allowed VaR to be a cornerstone of
"self-regulation." That this didn't work so well in 2008 was what
brought Alan Greenspan to his SOSD.

History has shown us not only that self-regulation is a dan-
gerous concept, attractive only to the gullible and the greedy, but
also that it is unwise to imagine a bank's condition can be usefully
summarized in a single number. Like RWA, loan-to-deposit ratio,
the leverage ratio, and all the rest of the regulatory ratios, VaR can
be a useful indicator of a bank's condition, especially if you can
get a series over some time. If a bank's VaR is moving in one direction or the other (and the movement wasn't from a change in
the underlying risk model) you can learn something about how
the bank is weathering the current market conditions. But you
can't elevate it to an importance above all the rest without inad-
vertently creating more risk than you can manage.

## Managing risk, and shedding it

What is the difference between managing risk and shedding it? In
the modern banking world, lending is often described as *originate-
and-distribute*, where a bank originates a loan, but then distributes
(sells) it to someone else to hold until it is paid off. The someone
else can be Fannie Mae, could be the FHLB, or could be the owner
of some mortgage-backed bond. Either way, the bank has sold the
risk to someone else. From the bank's perspective, shedding risk
is a sensible way to manage it.[82]

Before the advent of this model, "managing" risk involved either taking on less risk, or finding ways to make a particular loan
or set of loans less risky. A banker might do that by keeping track
of the borrower, either through other business he or she did with
the bank, or even socially. A borrower in trouble might be offered
an extension on a loan, or a refinance, or counseling into a smaller

---

[82]"Foisting" is sometimes a better term.

house and smaller loan. Another banker might decrease the risk of a loan to some business by helping that business find new markets, or better ways to reach familiar markets. They might offer a letter of credit on a borrower's behalf to expand business in distant markets. Failing all that, it's also possible for a banker to learn not to take certain risks again. These are all ways to manage credit risk. Some of these cost some money—maybe a loan at 5% had to be refinanced at 4%—and would presumably reduce a bank's profit. This is an old-fashioned way to do a bank's business.

With the newer model of managing risk by offloading, the profits stay high, and so does the risk, but someone else takes it. For example, in a climate of falling interest rates, a fixed-rate loan at 5% might be quite a valuable asset to sell, and a bank that sells it earns the sales price and removes the credit risk from their books. But when interest rates rise again, the buyer takes a loss. When managing risk just means offloading it, bankers make money on the way up and someone else loses it on the way down. This sounds clever, and in a way it is, but the result is that someone still has the risk and, without any contact with the original borrower, has no practical way to manage it beyond maybe finding a greater sucker.

While a bank has a relationship with its borrowers, the secondary buyer of a bank's loan has no relationship with the borrower. Even if the buyer wanted to manage the risk of the investment, it won't be possible for dozens of reasons, not least of which is the likely distance between the buyer and borrower. The bank takes the risk, but doesn't manage it in the old-fashioned sense, *so no one does*. The risk becomes systemic, because no one person or corporation is responsible. And because the originators bear no risk, they have no incentive to be careful. In other words, to the extent the originate-and-distribute model is widely adopted, the risk to the entire financial system goes up dramatically. And of course that's precisely what has happened.

Because shedding risk is a far less labor- and time-intensive way to manage it than the alternatives, banks have come up with a wide variety of ways to do exactly that. Mortgage bonds to offload credit risk are just the beginning. Interest rate swaps relieve a bank of interest rate risk, as do adjustable rate loans. Even a CD, with its fixed term, is a way to make a bank customer take a bank's liquidity risk.[83]  There are many more, both those known to regulators and doubtless more as yet undiscovered.

# Off-balance sheet activity

If you can't manage a risk, and can't get rid of it, another strategy is to hide it, and that brings us to assets and liabilities that are not recorded on a bank's balance sheet.

There is a category of asset and liability not recorded on a balance sheet, and called, oddly enough, *off-balance sheet*. This sounds somewhat underhanded, but there are legitimate reasons to account for things elsewhere than the balance sheet.  For example, if I sign a contract to loan $100 to you tomorrow, I have acquired an asset (the loan) in the sense that the contract is enforceable. But since the transaction hasn't happened, I don't actually have the asset, yet. A business line of credit works roughly this way, with the bank pre-approving a loan up to some limit which may or may not be reached.  Another example might be a bank that is managing not only its own assets, which appear on its balance sheet, but also providing management services for assets owned by its clients, which do not.  The assets it is managing (also called the *assets under management* or *AUM*) is a number important to anyone who wants to evaluate that aspect of the bank's business, but its relation to the balance sheet is complicated. A bank-sponsored money-market or stock fund will work this way. "Deposits" into such a fund are not liabilities of the bank, but investments held in trust for the customer.  The stock is owned by the customer, and so does not appear on the balance sheet. There is no resulting liability to the bank.

Operating leases are a very common off-balance sheet asset. A company might have a long-term lease of some asset. They don't own it, nor do they owe it to anyone else, but they *have* it. A bank, for example, might (probably does) lease the software that operates its account management system.  You won't find evidence of

---

[83]You risk running low on cash when you have too much tied up in a CD, but the bank doesn't.

operating leases on the balance sheet, but you might find it in the bank's income.[84]

Though there are plenty of legitimate reasons a bank might have off-balance sheet assets, there is a fair amount of judgment involved in deciding whether some assets belong on the balance sheet, and this provides plentiful opportunities for misdirection, deliberate obfuscation, and out-and-out fraud. There are a lot of variants to the less proper use of off-balance sheet accounting, but the basic idea of getting some asset off your balance sheet is to engineer some other entity that will coincidentally do whatever your company would have done with it. There might be some contractual relationship between the parent and spawn, or it might just be coincidence of decision makers. An entity created in order to do this is sometimes called a *special purpose entity* (*SPE*), or a *special interest vehicle* (*SIV*). You'll also hear *shell corporation*, but these are all more or less the same thing. According to the law, if this new SIV has any owners besides the founding corporation, its assets and liabilities might not have to be mentioned on the parent corporate balance sheet. The accounting standard has to do with the "certainty" that the asset or liability could eventually belong to the company. This is, as you can imagine, subject to a large helping of discretion.

Enron became famous among accountants for its use of off-balance sheet entities to hide its liabilities. They didn't invent the technique, but their use of it was so massive and elaborate, it might be appropriate to call them "pioneers." That is, Charles Lindbergh might have flown solo across the Atlantic first, but it was Juan Trippe, the founder of Pan Am, who made flying between the US and Europe commonplace. Think of Jeffrey Skilling, Enron's disgraced CEO, as the Juan Trippe of off-balance sheet accounting. Top Enron executives became partners in hundreds of SPEs in order to complicate their ownership and keep their liabilities off Enron's balance sheet.

The big issue with off-balance sheet activity is that there isn't

---

[84]Leases like this are a traditional form of tax avoidance, too. A company in New York might assign the ownership of its name and logo to a subsidiary based in the Bahamas, and lease the "intellectual property" for lease payments that are coincidentally equal to the company profits. Voila, that income has been moved from New York to the Bahamas, where it will thrive and grow, subject to Bahamian taxes (zero) instead of New York's (non-zero). Inventing a subsidiary like this in order to lease some asset back is called a *synthetic lease*.

really an easy-to-explain way to account for it all. What goes on a balance sheet is easy to define. What is relevant but not on the balance sheet is much murkier. As soon as an asset or liability is moved from the orderly and precise government of the balance sheet into the anarchy of off-balance sheet activity, the opportunities for abuse multiply like anarchic little rabbits.

In financial reports, these sorts of contractual obligations are supposed to appear somewhere—in the notes, or supplementary tables, or someplace. The Sarbanes-Oxley securities reform, adopted in the wake of the Enron debacle in 2002, dictated that any off-balance sheet activity be discussed in the 'Management Discussion and Analysis' section of a corporation's disclosure documents and that contractual obligations be listed in a table somewhere. But only a few years later, huge banks like Lehman Brothers were falling by the wayside from losses due to risks that never appeared in any disclosure documents.

It turned out there were loopholes. For example, the Sarbanes-Oxley rules included a clause exempting from disclosure investments where other parties bore the bulk of the risk. In 2007, State Street Bank held $28.8 billion in assets off its books because in the event of losses on those assets, other investors would be on the hook for the first $32 *million* in losses. These assets were technically owned by subsidiary "conduit" entities, and any losses greater than that would be State Street's. But their risk models confidently projected that there was little or no chance of losses exceeding that amount—a mere ninth of a percent of the value of the investment—so therefore other parties bore all the risk. Right? Predictably, these assets lost almost a billion dollars in value in 2008. All but a small fraction of that loss belonged to State Street, but none of that risk was apparent to anyone looking at their balance sheet.

For a bank, the process can work something like this: the bank creates an SIV and gets it some money, maybe by selling commercial paper, short-term IOUs with a fairly low interest rate. The SIV then buys loans from the bank, and resells them as mortgage-backed bonds. Because the operation isn't part of the bank and we're not talking about deposits, there are no reserve requirements, or loan loss reserves. Without having to put aside that money, the bank plus the SIV has a higher leverage than the bank alone did, and can therefore be more profitable. If they don't have to include the SIV's assets and liabilities on their balance sheet, regulators won't give them grief about it. A win-win situation, until things go bad, when it is demonstrated once again that while leverage is a great way to build a fortune, it is also a great way to destroy one.

Lehman Brothers used techniques like this to hide tens of billions of dollars in liabilities right up until it went bust in 2008. In fact, the unknown amount of liability squirreled away off Lehman's balance sheet was a factor in the last minute failure of the various bailout proposals: would-be rescuers were not at all sure what they would be rescuing. As of early 2013, JPMorgan Chase carried off-balance sheet assets, worth around $1.6 trillion. The assets on their actual balance sheet only add up to about $2.2 trillion, so the bank is significantly more leveraged than their balance sheet implies, since there's no such thing as "off-balance sheet capital."

Another tricky way to get assets off a bank's balance sheet is called *netting*. The idea is that in accounting for certain derivatives, the potential debts of one bank to another can cancel out. So if Bank A owes $5 million to Bank B, but B owes $6 million to A, then Bank A only needs to account for a $1 million asset and B a debt of the same amount. Both balance sheets have shrunk by $5 million, which will make their leverage seem smaller.[85] The problem with netting is that it doesn't account for the risk that one party will pay and the other will not. Bankruptcy proceedings, for example, would introduce risk of that sort into the mix, as would adjudication of the two debts by two different legal regimes, something that is quite easy to imagine in a world of international finance.

# The shadow banks

Consider an agency that originates student loans from bond funds. It is making loans direct to consumers, a traditional banking activity, but it takes no deposits, so it isn't a bank. Therefore

---

[85] This kind of accounting is only possible under the GAAP rules that prevail in the US. The International Financial Reporting Standards (IFRS), the accounting standard used for banks in Europe, do not permit this. Under those rules, JP-Morgan Chase, for example, has a leverage ratio below 5%, while under GAAP, it appears to be over 8%.

it has no reserve requirements, and probably has no regulator, either. It can take *all* the proceeds of a bond sale, or a repo transaction, and loan them out to college students. Without reserves, if there are any defaults among the student loans, the chance of being caught short is high. This agency is doing bank-like things, for better and worse, but isn't really a bank.

There are also all the SPEs and SIVs described above involved in holding assets off bank balance sheets. These are also not banks, and yet there they are, doing bank-ish things, like creating liquidity for mortgage lending. A money market fund, also not a bank, does not have "depositors," but it does have "investors" who expect to be able to withdraw their money at their own discretion, more or less. The names are different, but the function is economically similar. An investment bank that relies on short-term funding, like the repo market or its own commercial paper, to make longer-term credit available is doing the same thing, since its repo counterparties can always decline to roll over their loan.

All of these entities are involved in banking activities, to some extent. They are leveraging capital to provide credit, and simultaneously creating risk. Sometimes they manage it, but frequently just pass it off onto others. In a gross economic sense, they all have an effect on the supply of money in the economy, but none of them are regulated by the traditional bank regulators. This is is what got them the name of *shadow banks* (also called, more confusingly if less conspiratorially, the *non-bank banks*).

Not all forms of shadow banking are unregulated. The SEC, for example, oversees money market funds, though hedge funds and private equity funds, which can operate in pretty much the same way, are exempt from a host of regulations. But the regulations imposed by the SEC are more about issues like disclosure and transparency, less so about security, liquidity, and limits on risk-taking. The traditional concerns that bank regulators have for the health of the overall system are under-represented in the regulations of these entities. This is especially an issue given the tremendous growth in the shadow banks over the past decade. To say the least, the shadow banks remain an unsolved problem, and an ongoing threat to the stability of the financial system.

One important and widely overlooked point about the shadow banks is that much of what they do is made possible by actual banks. A money market fund that invests in mortgage bonds is using shareholder (depositor) money to make conventional bank loans possible. But the chances are very good that the fund is investing in the mortgages via an SIV set up to get loans off the balance sheet of some actual bank. The bank would not have set up the SIV without the money market fund right there to buy its bonds, and the money market fund would not be investing in mortgages but for the bank.

Some of the biggest and most threatening shadow banks worked this way in the run-up to the 2008 crisis. The banking industry frequently points to the shadow banks to say that if banks are not allowed to engage in some activity then the shadow banks will take up the slack. A more accurate picture might be to see much shadow banking activity as efforts by real banks to circumvent bank regulation. Since nothing has been done to rein in this activity, it all continues to this day.

# Information asymmetry

A great deal of bank risk can be attributed to what economists call *information asymmetry*. This is the situation when a buyer and seller of some item have very different levels of information about that item. The concept was pioneered by George Akerlof, whose 1970 paper, "The Market for Lemons: Quality Uncertainty and the Market Mechanism" made the point that when buyers of used cars know much less about them than sellers do, it will depress the price of even the excellent used cars. Akerlof, along with Joseph Stiglitz and Michael Spence, won the 2001 Economics Nobel for work elaborating this observation, but like a lot of things economists "know" there's a long way between the theory and useful public policy.

For example, a bank knows more than a depositor ever could about the financial strength of the bank and about what's really hidden inside all that fine print. On the flip side, of course, the borrower knows more than the bank ever can about the likelihood of any particular loan being repaid. A great deal of the financial crisis of 2008 was attributable to information asymmetry:

- Buyers of mortgage-backed bonds knew almost nothing about the mortgages backing those bonds;

- Ratings agencies were making the problem worse by debasing their reputations, and accepting fees from the issuers for their ratings, an obvious conflict of interest for agencies supposedly working on behalf of the buyers;

- Mortgage brokers promoted Alt-A, also called liar loans, *no-doc* loans and *NINJA* (No Income, No Job or Assets) loans, where the lenders knew very little about the borrowers;

- The balance sheets of the big banks became so opaque, and off-balance sheet assets so prevalent, that shareholders and potential buyers of bank stocks couldn't tell what was going on inside them.

An information-asymmetric transaction provides huge challenges for the party with less information, since the prospects of being cheated are substantial. What's more, the same transaction presents a huge moral risk for the party with more information. This is why the reputation of a used-car salesman is important: it has actual cash value to that salesman, since a good reputation means getting a better price for a car.

Banks, whose solvency depends on the confidence of their customers, have shown over decades of experience that they cannot be trusted with their own reputations, and that's where bank regulators come into the picture.

*Five*

# Starting a bank

I T IS ALTOGETHER TOO EASY to see what's wrong with banking today. It is much harder to decide what to do about it. Since so much of what has gone wrong is a failure of regulation,[86] it is natural to propose better regulations. This, of course, has been tried, and those better regulations are being written now—and being fought tooth and nail by well-paid bank lobbyists. Certainly more must be done in this space, but one potential avenue to reform that has not received a lot of attention is to fight back by starting a bank, or some other institution, to provide financial services in a better and more responsible way.

Traditionally, starting a bank is something for rich investors to do, but there are plenty of other parties out there who have the capacity to have an impact on our financial system. You might be a county supervisor or a city official, upset by the poor treatment your government gets from its bank. You might be involved with a union, or work at a company where a credit union or mutual bank could thrive. Or you might see a business niche for a responsible financial service provider, and have the capacity to find investors to back it.[87] Any of these will move the financial reform ball forward a few inches, and that's what is most important.

To start a bank, all you need are two things: some money and a plan. They are equally important. If anything, the plan is the more important, since that usually helps you get the money, while having money wthout a plan usually means losing the money. Along the way you need to put together a board of directors, get approval from regulators, establish operating procedures and sys-

---

[86] And failure of self-regulation. Remember Alan Greenspan's SOSD.

[87] Of course, you might also be intent on exploiting your community and cashing out after your first billion. In that case, I hope you paid full price for this book.

tems, but those all come much later. Plan first.

What is a plan? It's a goal, and a means to get there. There are a lot of banks, why should a new one exist? This is not a rhetorical question; it's easy to come up with reasons. Your job is to pick one (or two or three) and make them the focus of the institution you are attempting to create. Are you attempting to serve a particular area? A particular group of people? A government? Do you have reason to suspect your future customers aren't satisfied with the banks they already have access to? Is the service your bank will provide going to be better, fairer, cheaper, faster, easier? More honest?

Having a purpose will help you focus your efforts, and it will also help muster support for your project. This support might take the form of investors, people willing to put in sweat equity, city council members or county supervisors considering whether a public-owned financial institution makes sense, or something else. Banking involves a certain amount of risk and work, so the claim that having a bank because it's a Good Thing is unlikely to sway as many people as a sharper focus will.

Once you have a goal, it's time to assemble the plan. This will involve choosing the kind of bank you think will work— wholesale, retail? commercial or savings? credit union? funded how? serving who?—and designing it to fit the conditions of your market. You'll find yourself talking to investors and regulators. Perhaps these will be officials of a county or town or school district,[88] and perhaps they will be other like-minded people. You'll have other decisions to make, such as whether you're seeking a state or national charter. You'll start to assemble a budget and financial projections, to refine the plan, and then it's time to get it funded and get underway.

---

[88]One suggestion: when talking with regulators, or with any official on whose approval your project hinges, don't ever ask, "Is this legal?" If you ask a simple question about a proposal on a subject unfamiliar to them and they say no, then your whole effort risks being shut down before it even begins. Ask instead, "Here's our goal; what are the limitations we face while trying to achieve it?" This is especially important when talking to a legal authority, like a city solicitor, whose opinion will be binding, at least for some time.

# Early decisions

Among the important decisions to make early on is what kind
of charter to seek. The choice of whether to be chartered by a
state or federal government will also decide questions like which
regulators will be involved, and how many of them.

You'll also have to choose whether you're talking about a commercial bank or a savings bank. Or a credit union or something
else. There were once significant differences between commercial
and savings banks. One was to service business, the other grew
up more to serve individuals. With deregulation, the two types
of bank have been growing steadily more similar over the past
30 years, and at this point, the only real difference is one of em-
phasis: a savings bank is supposed to concentrate on consumer
lending and is expected to have about 70% of its loan portfolio in
real estate lending.[89]

Once you've decided on your goal, the choice of commercial
or savings bank is relatively easy to make. The choice of national
or state charter is a little cloudier. The differences are complex and
it's not easy to say what the advantages are or are not. The regulatory costs are generally higher for a national charter, but again the
differences are complex. If you plan to focus on a particular city,
county, or state, and especially if the plan involves government
sponsorship or ownership, it seems natural to be chartered by the
state. However, on further analysis that choice may seem only
aesthetic. There is probably no substitute for modeling your plan
and making the choice once you've constructed some of the financial projections, and consulted with regulators with your plan in
hand.

The other important step worth taking at this point is to recon-
sider your purpose and think hard about whether there's a way
to achieve it that does not involve a bank charter. Maybe your
goal only requires a trust company, an investment company, or
an investment bank? Treasury licenses something called a Community Development Financial Institution (CDFI) (see "Beef up
a CDFI" on page 151), which is more of a role than a definition.

---

[89]The federal thrift charter was in danger of being abolished during the negoti-
ations over the Dodd-Frank legislation in 2010. The charter still exists, but Dodd-
Frank pretty much eliminated the advantages the charter had over the commercial
bank charter, without significantly broadening the lending restrictions on a thrift.
In other words, the charter still exists, but why would you want one?

Some CDFI's are banks and credit unions, and some are just loan programs, revolving funds, or venture capital funds, allowed to do bank-like things (like access the FHLB) without actually being a bank. A bank can do many interesting things, and a commercial or savings charter can definitely be worth pursuing, but consider if it is possible to do what you hope this institution will do without the risk and regulatory overhead of full-scale banking. Or if you can, why not form the institution now, achieve a short-term goal that does not require a bank charter, and maybe encourage your board to seek a charter somewhere down the road? Banking can be a harsh business, and there's some reason to think an institution that has already developed some organizational strength and a record of success—perhaps may already have a portfolio of performing loans—will have a better chance to succeed as a bank.

If you get past that hurdle, another point to consider is whether you are forming a bank or a bank and a holding company that will contain it. (Or maybe just the holding company.) A holding company can provide some useful flexibility if there are multiple goals and some don't involve banking. A holding company can also be used to address control issues. For example, a mutually-owned holding company can keep control of a bank among a small set of founders while a mutual bank will potentially be controlled by its depositors. If you want the benefits of mutual ownership, but not the risk of loss of control, a holding company can make sense. On the downside, a holding company has more overhead, another regulator (the Fed supervises bank holding companies), and more complexity.

## Thinking like a banker

One of the lessons bankers learn is that things look different from within the bank than from the outside, and this is worth bearing in mind as you consider possible business ideas. Take The Bancorp bank of Delaware, for example. It was originally established to do merchant processing of credit cards. At inception, it took no deposits at all, but simply managed the payments coming from consumers to stores, via credit cards. It takes a certain amount of time for payments to settle out, so that at any one time, Bancorp had a few hundred million dollars in transit, and the loans they made came right from that fund.

From outside the bank, each merchant sees money arrive in their bank account in a matter of a day or two after the credit card purchase. None of them will perceive the money in transit from their customer to them as being loanable. The very idea would seem silly. From inside the bank, however, the "account" that has all those funds passing through looks like a single large pool of money, with roughly equivalent amounts of money flowing in and out of it each day in a more or less predictable fashion. From the outside perspective, making loans from that money might seem crazy, while from the inside it makes perfect sense.

When looking for banking opportunities, one can't just consider static piles of money. Places where money flows through are equally important. A pension fund, for example, represents a large pool of money. The legions of bankers and financiers attracted to those pools is legendary. But putting the pension fund itself aside for the moment, every pension manager has a bank account out of which checks are written to retirees each month. That account will typically hold a substantial balance because checks take a certain time to clear, even direct-deposit checks. The money appears to be flowing through, but there is always a lot in there, and that's something a bank can and will use.

# What does a bank do with its capital?

For a bank that's up and running, the "capital" is largely an abstraction. In an accounting sense, it is just the component of the bank's assets that don't have to be paid back. In the financial sense, it's the assets a bank can afford to lose without sacrificing customer money or closing its doors.

For a bank that's starting up, however, the capital is the stake with which everything begins. Before it begins operations, the capital is typically used to pay the legal expenses of getting the bank charter, the initial expenses of setting up the account management software, and buy the furniture. It's not unusual to pay managers during the staffing-up period, either. How the accountants choose to record these expenses is up to their interpretation, but in an accounting sense, the assets purchased here, some of which are intangible, all wind up balanced against numbers on the capital side of the ledger.

Up until, and including, the day a bank opens its doors, the capital is all it has to pay every one of its expenses: rent, salaries, opening a reserve account at the Fed, cash in the vault, and the supply of toasters to give new customers. Some of the capital is hopefully also used to make the first loans, in order to begin persuading income to flow in the door. If you start with deposits only, you risk paying money right away instead of making it. However, modern banks, for better and (frequently) worse, have come to rely heavily on fee income from depositors, so there is typically income from the liability side of the balance sheet, too.

As we saw with the Sunnydale bank's start, some of the expenses from a bank's startup capital are never going to return to the bank in monetary form. Some of the expenses will be for assets that have value: bonds, art, buildings, and so on. But many expenses will be money spent that is not coming back. On the asset side of the bank's balance sheet, these will find their ways to various intangible categories, like good will or customer and supplier relationships, trademarks, and rights to this or that. Other expenses, such as furniture or renovations will find their way into capital assets, until they're eased off the balance sheet via depreciation allowances. When regulators subtract the value of intangible assets from a bank's capital (as in the calculation of Tier 1 capital) they're attempting to estimate how much of a bank's accounting capital isn't really money. However, it's worth noting that all they get this way is an estimate.

# Making a bank's business plan

To proceed with any kind of banking plan, you will find it essential to assemble a business plan. The bad news is that it is a lot of work, but the good news is that there is plenty of guidance available.

A business plan is a record of the planning you've done and the road you intend to follow. The plan should be extensive, not because it's important to type a lot of words, but because the planning really ought to be extensive, too. If you haven't thought about how your bank will deal with interest rate risk, it's better to do it now, when you're tossing around imaginary dollars, than later, when you have the responsibility for real dollars.

The first step is, in many ways, the hardest, and that is settling on a goal. What are you hoping to do with this bank? Are you thinking about serving the unbanked? Helping a city free itself from the oppression of the bond market? Enhancing access to business credit in some area? Undermining expensive payday lenders? None of the above? All of the above? Advice about making a business plan is like instructions for driving a car: it's all important information to know, but it's not going to tell you where you want to go. You're the one who decides that, and the rest is guidance for getting you there safely and in style. Without a goal, you'll find yourself stumped for answers while you try to work out a business plan. With a goal, many of the questions will almost answer themselves.

These are some other decisions you'll have to make while you put together a business plan. The place to begin is to try to imagine what kind of infrastructure you'll need to support the function you've decided on—how many people, what services are done in house and which are not, where housed—and that will help you understand what kinds of margins you'll have to build into the business.

## Industry vendors do what?

While designing your bank, one thing to be aware of is that over the past thirty years, all kinds of industries in America have outsourced all kinds of services. This has had some seriously unpleasant economic effects on our nation, but you can use it to your advantage, since your brand-new bank can purchase the same software service the big banks use and therefore provide service every bit as good, secure, and fast as theirs. For a substantial portion of the services your bank is to provide, you may be able to identify an industry vendor that can provide it. Which way you go here will depend a great deal on what you're trying to do, but spend some time identifying vendor roles—account management software,[90] courier, lockbox, cleaning, watering the plants, choosing art for the branches, whatever—and see if there's a vendor in that niche.

---

[90]This is an important one. There are a few big names in this market and a bunch of smaller ones. This market evolves constantly, so it's not practical to list them here, but they're not hard to find. Call them up, make friends with their sales team, get a demo, don't promise anything yet.

Because the 21st century has no bottom to its capacity to as-
tonish, there are consulting firms who dispense advice to banks
on cash management and investments, customer relations, and
market conditions. That is, parts of the industry even appear
to have outsourced management decisions, though one wonders
how many forego the executives themselves. There are even vendors (the private-label banks we met under "Banker's bank" on
page 71) who supply the whole bank; you can just put your own
name on the front door and be done with it.[91]

For any of these service suppliers, don't be afraid to contact
the sales team and get information. Being pleasant, at least for a
while, to interesting people who call with funny ideas that might
earn them money is part of their job description.

## Consulting the authorities

If you haven't already, go spend some quality time on the FDIC
and OCC web sites. They are a wealth of guidance for both current and future bank directors. You'll find memos about liquidity
risk management and how to write a charter and bylaws, booklets about how to recruit directors and how to put together an annual report. Among the more useful documents you'll find are a
few different versions of guidelines for putting together a business
plan. They were written for slightly different audiences and by
slightly different agencies (the Office of Thrift Supervision (OTS)
was merged with OCC) and emphasize slightly different issues.
You can do worse than to spend the time to read them all.

My favorite booklet on the OCC site is the OTS document 625
"Business Plan Guidelines" from the "Thrift Application Handbook" and still residing at www.occ.gov (look under "Publications" and then "Licensing Manuals"), because it is quite explicit
about what is expected and what you will need to do. It would be
hard for a little book like the one you are reading to do any better,
so go read it.[92]

---

[91]There's an online bank called Simple.com, started by an entrepreneur less
interested in actual banking than simply in having a convenient and modern place
for consumers to keep their money. Simple is essentially a software company that
makes and runs the front-end, customer-facing, software for their bank. You can't
go to them for a loan. The actual money is kept in real banks who provide banking
service (and deal with the regulators) so Simple can pretend to be a bank.

[92]On www.occ.gov, look for the Comptroller's Handbook Booklets, and the
"Topics" heading. On the FDIC site, at www.fdic.gov, look for the "Resources for

As you begin to fill out each section of your business plan, click around on the sites to find relevant memos and booklets. If you're trying to make something new and better than an existing bank model (and I hope you are), you won't find anything perfectly appropriate, but you will find documents that describe the sorts of concerns regulators will have. Regulators are, after all, one of the intended audiences for your plan.

You should work on the financial projections in parallel with the business plan. Problems you find in one will inform what you put into the other. It is a waste of time to write about stuff that won't work, especially when the arithmetic will tell you so. Save yourself some time and work on them together.

Somewhere around a quarter of the way through the planning process, after you've made your list of research topics, laid out your financial projections and begun to fill them in, but before you complete your first draft, call up the FDIC or OCC or the banking regulators in your state, and make a date to chat about your project. It is wise to engage the regulators early and as often as etiquette and their schedules will permit. By calling the regulators you will connect with people interested in banking and if perhaps not quite eager to hear about new ideas, still willing to engage and hear them out.[93] Many regulators are well aware of the shortcomings in the current banking market, and are as likely as anyone to have useful suggestions about overcoming them, provided they are speaking to someone who knows what they're talking about and is prepared.

# Financial projections

The most important part of a bank business plan is the purpose, but the second most important is the financial projections. The written plan describes what you're going to do, but the projections say why it's going to work.

When you first see a finished page of projections, it can seem intimidating, but there's a relatively simple formula for putting one together, and the rest is just time and attention.

---

Officers & Directors" and the "Director's Resource Center." (As of October 2013.)

[93]Remember, they're regulators, whose words have legal weight, so they can't very well say, "what a good idea" to an application, but if you listen carefully, you'll hear encouragement if you deserve it.

1. Create a spreadsheet page for your assumptions. This is everything, from the number of customers you expect, to the amounts you expect each to have on deposit or to borrow. Give each assumption a row, and give yourself time increments in the columns. You'll want to do the first three years in quarters, but after that, annual is plenty. The first column is opening day, and the subsequent columns represent the *end* of each period.

|   | A | B | C | D | E | F | G | H |
|---|---|---|---|---|---|---|---|---|
| 1 |   |   | Year 1 |   |   |   | Year 2 |   |
| 2 |   | Open | Q1 | Q2 | Q3 | Q4 | Q1 | Q2 |
| 3 | loan interest % | 4.0 | 4.0 | 4.1 | 4.2 | 4.2 | 4.3 | 4.3 |
| 4 | account interest % | 0.2 | 0.2 | 0.2 | 0.2 | 0.2 | 0.2 | 0.3 |
| 5 | rent |   |   |   |   |   |   |   |

2. Lay out your balance sheet. This will have balance sheet items as its rows, and the same column headings as the assumptions page. Fill in the first column with what you expect to have on opening day and make sure it balances (A = C + L). Look for an existing financial report on the OCC or FDIC site, and use the same labels, or at least the ones that are appropriate for your project.

|   | A | B | C | D | E | F | G | H |
|---|---|---|---|---|---|---|---|---|
| 1 | ($ thousands) |   | Year 1 |   |   |   | Year 2 |   |
| 2 |   | Open | Q1 | Q2 | Q3 | Q4 | Q1 | Q2 |
| 3 | demand deposits | 1,000 |   |   |   |   |   |   |
| 4 | loans outstanding | 0 |   |   |   |   |   |   |
| 5 | loan-loss allowance | 0 |   |   |   |   |   |   |

3. Lay out an income statement. This will be a statement of how much is earned (or lost) in each period. Most of the quantities in this statement will be derived from numbers in your assumptions and numbers on the opening column of the balance sheet. For example, the interest expense will be the interest rate you pay on deposits, which ought to be in your assumptions, times the total amount of deposits, which ought to be a line on the balance sheet.[94]

---

[94]It can be a little confusing, but I usually put these on the same spreadsheet page as the balance sheet, in order to avoid switching from one page to another, but choose your own favorite way to work.

|   | A | B | C | D | E | F | G | H |
|---|---|---|---|---|---|---|---|---|
| 1 | ($ thousands) |   | Year 1 | | | | Year 2 | |
| 2 |   |   | Q1 | Q2 | Q3 | Q4 | Q1 | Q2 |
| 3 | interest expense |   | 2 |   |   |   |   |   |
| 4 | interest earned |   | 0 |   |   |   |   |   |
| 5 | rent paid |   | 100 |   |   |   |   |   |

4. The entries on the income statement will then go back into adjustments to the balance sheet rows, creating the next column out. For example, if you pay interest on the deposits, presumably the deposit base will grow by the amount of interest plus whatever new deposits you expect that quarter. Here, you will have to make some policy decisions, like how much of the earnings will remain in capital and how much paid to the shareholders. Will you grow loans first, or focus on growing deposits first? What kinds of funding can you expect to find early on? Make some decisions and rough them into the appropriate section of your business plan, but also make sure they're recorded as assumptions on the assumption page.

|   | A | B | C | D | E | F | G | H |
|---|---|---|---|---|---|---|---|---|
| 1 | ($ thousands) |   | Year 1 | | | | Year 2 | |
| 2 |   | Open | Q1 | Q2 | Q3 | Q4 | Q1 | Q2 |
| 3 | demand deposits | 1,000 | 2,000 |   |   |   |   |   |
| 4 | loans outstanding | 0 | 50 |   |   |   |   |   |
| 5 | loan-loss allowance | 0 | 2.5 |   |   |   |   |   |

5. After you fill in the first column of the balance sheet, go back and make sure it balances. In most spreadsheet programs, there isn't a way to do this automatically without writing your own macros, so unless you're a macro writer, do be careful here. Creating a spreadsheet that doesn't balance can lead you to believe you've discovered cold fusion—a safe and secure bank that is also highly profitable—and can lead to embarrassing moments down the line when you show it to someone more knowledgable than you are. It's an instant credibility killer. Balance the sheet by choosing a row ("shareholder's equity" is a good one) to adjust up or down each quarter or year. Include a row that sums the total Assets, Liabilities, and Capital, so you can see a row of zeroes as a check that all is well.

6. Make another column in your income lines, and then another in the balance sheet, rinse and repeat until you've predicted at least three, but better five or even ten years.

7. Now look at the bottom line: **will this bank survive?** Is there enough income to support it? This is the hard part, because if you've been honest during the construction of the spreadsheet, your bottom line is almost certainly negative some years out from the opening. This can be a problem, because the assumptions you've made are almost certainly rosy ones. That's what everyone does. Plus you probably forgot to incorporate the loan-loss allowance, because almost everyone does that on the first pass, too. Remember that the banking rule of thumb is that a de novo bank loses money for the first three years. You need to judge whether that kind of loss is viable in your circumstances, as well as whether it eventually turns positive.

8. Start hunting through your spreadsheet to identify the assumptions and events that are the most important for creating that loss and see if they can be addressed somehow. Can you plausibly lower the interest rate you pay on deposits? Can you plausibly raise the rate you earn on loans? Can you do either without destroying your bank's reason for existing? Is there some other source of income you can claim? Are there too many employees? Are you using a high or low number for salaries and benefits?

9. If you can't answer these questions in a plausible way to make the numbers positive, try to think of all the people you told about this project and how to live your life without running into them again until they've forgotten about it. Then quietly forget about it yourself.

10. If you can answer them and find a plausible way to make your project succeed, then congratulations. Go record the assumptions and policy decisions that made it work in your business plan.

*Six*

# Basic government finance

GOVERNMENT FINANCE is a vast world of taxes, bonds, and creative financing schemes. There's nothing really basic about it, to be honest. A short book like this can only point at most of the subject, but since this is actually a book about banks, we can view some of the features of governments through that lens and just talk about the parts of government that are relevant to bankers.[95]

1. First and foremost: A lot of money flows through governments. Even nearly bankrupt cities collect and disburse millions of dollars in taxes each year.

2. The money that flows through does so on a tremendous volume of transactions. Lots of small deposits in, lots of paychecks and other comparably-sized checks out. The liquidity demands can be high.

3. Accountability and audit demands are high. Federal funding sources, like HUD or the Dept of Education, have fairly demanding audit requirements. Recipient governments have to keep granted funds separate, and they use elaborate accounting or even separate bank accounts to do so.

4. On the whole, governments are very risk-averse. Most of the financial blowups that have plagued cities and counties over the past few years stemmed from misbegotten attempts to *reduce* risk, or at least to trade one kind of risk for another.

---

[95]Apart from the fact that many bankers appear to view their local state or municipal government as marks to be fleeced, see "Predatory public finance" on page 137.

5. Finances are relatively predictable. Through the course of a year, a government usually has a pretty good idea of the gross movements of money. Even when economic conditions create a funding crisis, they have usually been predicted months in advance.

6. Governments are big borrowers. It is quite typical for them to depend heavily on borrowing for both their day-to-day and long-term operations. The flip side of having a highly predictable income stream is that you don't have much flexibility. Expensive infrastructure projects must be amortized over several years. Consequently, virtually all governments in the US borrow heavily. A government can borrow either from banks or from the open bond market, and both are routine.

These are some of the constraints on handling government funds. As deposits, the cost of funds (to the bank) is relatively high, and there are a large number of transactions to process. On the positive side, there is a lot of money there, it's highly predictable, and the governments are big and reliable debtors.[96]

Any banking proposal that anticipates using public funds, whether as a customer or an investor, is going to have to account for these realities in order to be taken seriously by the legislators, executives, bankers, or regulators whose approval is important. It also has to take into account the fact that as of this writing (2013), bond yields and other interest rates are at their historic rock-bottom. This makes the cost of funds low, which sounds good, but the flip side is that it also makes for very low bank revenue. A bank getting underway now will find it difficult to cover its operating costs in the near term. It's a good time to *have* a bank, but a lousy time to start one. On the upside, if, despite the low rates, you can come up with a design that makes sense, it will do much better in years to come.

---

[96]Much more reliable than the ratings agencies would have you believe. The risk of default for any municipal bond is far lower than for any comparably-rated corporate bond. The state of Connecticut sued S&P, Moody's, and Fitch for exactly this, accusing them of systematically (and purposefully) overestimating the risk of default on municipal bonds issued by Connecticut cities and towns, costing them hundreds of millions in increased interest costs. The credit agencies settled in 2011.

# Budgets and financial reports

The two key financial documents for any government are its budget and its financial reports. The budget is an account of spending to be done in the future, and the financial report is a record of what actually happened. Thinking about the government in terms that a banker might, you can see the budget as a record of what the government plans (or hopes) to do, and the financial report as an account of the money with which to do it.

The first thing to bear in mind when looking over these documents is that most governments are actually pretty complicated. A city will be not only the city, but also the water department, the sewer fund, the parking authority, the redevelopment agency, and more—except in other cities where it's the sewer department, the water fund, the redevelopment authority, the parking agency, and more. And maybe also the school department, housing authority, parks department,[97] museum, airport, hospital, golf course, zoo, scenic caverns, beaches, and, well, you get the picture. These are organized differently in virtually every town, city, county, or state in the country.

Roughly speaking, though, these entities can be separated into three categories, which is what the accountants do.

**Government and its subdivisions.** These are departments of the government, or other entities under the direct control of the leaders, the way the city clerk's office is under the Mayor.

**Business-type activities.** These are government services provided for some kind of fee. They can (probably are) subsidized by tax dollars to some degree, but are substantially supported by those fees, or some kind of revenue that makes it resemble a business. In turn, a business-type activity could be an *enterprise fund* for services provided to the public, or an *internal service fund*, for service available to other components of the government. A landfill supported by tipping fees for dumping trash might be organized as an enterprise fund, while an audit function, whose fees are expenses of the departments it audits, might be an internal service fund. Enterprise funds are sometimes called *proprietary funds*.

---

[97]Often constituted separately from the rest of the city to prevent mayors from selling off park land.

**Associated agency.** Many governments will have associated authorities or corporations that are not an official part of the government, but carry out government functions. A redevelopment authority, for example, might do economic development lending in a county. It might be legally separate from the county, but have its board appointed by county supervisors.

A government's budget documents will typically cover all the first category, and maybe some of the business-type activities, though it will seldom mention these categories, which are accounting terms. The financial report, if it has the word "consolidated" in its title, should have all of the business-type activities in it, with the government, and being a report prepared by accountants, will use the accounting terms. Typically, neither one will contain information for the associated agencies, which will report and budget separately, though there are exceptions.

One important distinction among these different categories is that they are probably funded with different sources of revenue, and those sources will ebb and flow at different times throughout a fiscal year. Income tax collections, for example, peak in April and May each year, no matter what the withholding rules say. Property tax collections tend to peak after the first bill of the year is sent out. Sales tax collections peak in December and January, and zoo admissions peak during school vacations. Other sources are more consistent. Sewer bills, for example, tend to be relatively steady, as do building permits, at least in warm climates. The ebb and flow of such funds is usually not part of a budget or a financial report,[98] but it is important information for the government's own cash managers, as well as its bankers.

## Budgets

A government's budget documents describe the spending plan for a fiscal year. They usually lay out the departments and the dollars to be spent on each one. There is usually a piece of legislation that constitutes the appropriation for the budget, and a document describing what's in the legislation. The legislation isn't usually that informative to outsiders, though it is the more authoritative document.

---

[98]Though many governments will issue monthly or quarterly financial reports that will contain clues to the fluctuation.

Do remember, when you're looking at a budget, that it is a prediction of the future, and therefore is just a guess, even if it's an educated guess. All budgets are eventually proven wrong, though of course some are more wrong than others. Most budget documents will include numbers from previous years, and those can be a better guide to reality. Budgets are issued prospectively, to outline spending for the upcoming year, so the "previous" budget year in the most recent budget available is probably the year you're in right now, so that one has some guesswork, too. If you're reading the budget for fiscal year 2015, you're probably only part of the way through fiscal year 2014. The numbers for fiscal year 2013 will be real (they might say "actual" or "audited" on them) but any year after that contains at least some guesswork.

Budgets vary widely in their coverage of a government's component entities. Some governments will include in the budget all their business-type activities, and also their associated agencies. Others will include only the government departments, or the government departments and *some* enterprise funds, and they will seldom identify the funds that way in a budget. For some governments, you won't get a picture of what's going on without consulting several different budget documents, for each of the government's component units.

There aren't really any good standards for budgets and budget presentations, so they vary widely in quality and information. They do tend to have some concepts in common, and here's a desultory list of useful concepts.

**General fund.** A government's *general fund* is money that can be spent on any expense the government incurs. Most taxes will go into the general fund, to be dispersed according to the whim of the legislative body and executive in charge.

**Restricted funds.** Much of the money a government receives is earmarked for some specific expense. Unemployment taxes, for example, typically are restricted to spending on unemployment benefits. Tuition to a public community college will be restricted to be used at the college. Federal contributions to some program will be restricted to that program, and grant funds restricted to the purposes outlined in the original proposal.

**Budget reserve.** Many governments won't budget all the money they expect to receive. Frequently they'll budget 98% of the expected income, and call the remaining 2% the *budget reserve* and include that item in the presentation, so the expenses add up to the revenues. Depending on the optimism of the budget assumptions, this money may or may not actually exist. Either way, it isn't correct to think of this as a pool of money sitting around. If a government with a budget reserve is lucky enough to collect more than 98% of its taxes and has budgeted its expenses correctly, there will be money left over, and it's likely that some will find its way into a cash reserve, which can be a source of confusion between the two. It's typical to appropriate budget reserve funds—if they exist—for maintenance of capital assets, or paying down debt issues, or something else discretionary.

**Cash reserve.** Also called a *rainy day fund*, a *cash reserve* is a pool of money intended to be tapped in an emergency. For some governments, this kind of emergency happens every year, and the cash reserve is a pad intended to get the government over its low-cash moments. You can't really call a cash reserve truly without restrictions until you know about the ebb and flow of funds throughout the fiscal year.

When trying to analyze the financial state of a government, or to determine exactly what assets it has available, you should also be interested in any kind of capital planning documents that might be out there. Sometimes these will be an appendix to a budget, or included in it, but only sometimes. These will account for the government's planned capital expenses over the next few years. Many of these expenses will require borrowing funds, so they are essentially predictions of moments when the government will need a bank. The capital planning documents or the budget will often have a record of past borrowing. There are also usually other useful documents that might contain clues about capital plans: transportation planning documents, water and sewer resource guides, landfill annual reports, and so on.

One final point about budget documents. The first time you go through one, you'll likely find yourself somewhat disappointed. You'll see some budgeted dollar amount, but the document won't say how it is spent or on what (or to whom) except in the vaguest fashion. In truth, there are very few truly interesting questions that most budget documents can answer. Treat a budget document as a way to learn what the interesting questions *are*, and to equip yourself to have an intelligent conversation with officials, but understand that you will probably need to answer those deeper questions in some other way than reading the budget.

## Financial reports

The other important document for a government is its annual financial report. Also called a *CAFR* for "Comprehensive Annual Financial Report," this document is an account of what the government actually did during a fiscal year. Unlike a budget document, it's a record of what happened, instead of an account of what is planned. The Governmental Accounting Standards Board (*GASB*) issues guidelines for what should go into a CAFR, so these are much more uniform than budget documents. The CAFR will include all the enterprise funds and internal service funds in its presentation. That's what makes it a "Comprehensive" report.

For each component of the government, including its funds, you should see the following:

- An *asset statement*, or *statement of net assets*, which are alternate accounting terms for a balance sheet. On these, you'll find numbers for the capital assets (net of debt), restricted assets that can only be used for some specific purpose, and unrestricted assets, that can be used for any (legal) purpose. The bottom line for a government will be its *fund balance* or *net assets*, which is roughly like a bank's capital, in that it isn't necessarily money, just the difference between the assets and liabilities. When you see that some town has a fund balance of $10 million, it probably doesn't mean that $10 million is sitting around somewhere.

- An income statement, accounting for changes in the assets by identifying the different sources of revenue and expenses. The bottom line—whether the government had a surplus or deficit—is on this statement.

- A statement of cash flow. This is related to the income statement, except that the categories reported are not the sources of revenue and expenses (like "property tax" or "sewer user fees") but kinds of revenue and expenses ("payments to suppliers" or "payments to employees").

For a banker, it's worth knowing how much of all this represents cash and investments. Cash appears in the "current assets" line in the asset statement, which is usually expanded somewhere. The cash flow statement can be useful, too.

Somewhere near these tables, you should see a line reading something to the effect of this:

"The notes to this financial statement are integral to the financial statement."

This is a true statement. The notes are often the most revealing part. Read them, if only for the entertainment value. This is where the accountants let loose with their opinions about what they're reporting. They don't use exclamation points ever, but you can find outrage and incredulity between the lines of the notes, if deserved.

The CAFR should also contain an accounting of debt issues, past and anticipated. There is plenty more in most CAFRs, but those are the items of interest to most bankers. Do remember that the CAFR will contain the proprietary funds, but it may not mention the associated agencies and authorities that also make up a government's operation. That is, in one city it might account for the sewer fund (money to run the sewers funded by sewer fees) but in another city it might not account for the sewer authority (an independent entity that does exactly same thing). There is, it seems, no limit to how differently two cities can organize precisely the same activity.

Something else you'll notice when you troll through a CAFR is that it is usually almost impossible to reconcile the finances as reported in the CAFR with the finances proposed in the budgets. There are blessed exceptions out there, but the two reports tend to use different categories and report on different collections of funds. When comparing one fiscal year to another, it is safest to compare financial report numbers to financial report numbers and budget numbers to budget numbers. Don't mix them unless you are absolutely sure you know what's what.

# Pension funds

Somewhere in the documents outlining a government's finances, there will probably be information about one or more pension systems. These might be part of the government accounts, or they might be in some free-standing trust. It is the unusual government that is not behind in its payments, partly because pension funds are a relatively new development, partly because of new pension accounting rules put out in the 1990s, and partly because governments are just like that. The same is also true of *other post-employment benefit (OPEB)* accounting, also known as health benefits for retirees.

There isn't nearly enough room in this book for a real discussion of pension accounting, the way that governments are being forced to apply them, or the angst and devastation these accounting rules have caused, in many cases needlessly. Suffice to say that protections enacted in the private sector to protect retirees against businesses ceasing to exist make little sense in the public sector, and yet that's what GASB insists be done. Putting that debate aside, here are some basic terms you will find useful in discussions of pension funds, pension benefits and OPEB funding.

A pension fund's liability is typically taken to be the *present value* of all the benefits it will pay in the future. The present value is the amount of money that, when invested at some reasonable rate of return, will provide those payments in the future. For example, the present value of $105 a year from now at a *discount rate* of 5% is $100. At a higher discount rate, the present value is lower, so at a rate of 10%, the present value of $105 is $95.45. Naturally, for a pension fund with many beneficiaries of all different ages, this can be a pretty complicated calculation; that's what actuaries do with their time.

The key number in pension accounting is the *unfunded liability*, also called the *UAAL* (the A's stand for "actuarially accrued"). This is a comparison between the present value of all the benefits to be paid in the future and the money actually on hand. If the actuaries calculate that the city of Sunnydale will need $1 billion to meet its future retirement benefits, and it only has $700 million on hand in the pension fund, that's an unfunded liability of $300 million. This is also commonly expressed as a *funding ratio* of 70%.

As you can imagine, the UAAL is sensitive to assumptions about the discount rate, about the population of employees and retirees, and to the number of years into the future the accountants think the funding should go. Thirty years is typical, but this varies.[99] All of these choices are quite controversial among actuaries and accountants, who argue with each other about issues like these all the time, but get touchy when laymen weigh in.

The other important pension accounting number useful for reading budgets is the *actuarially required contribution*, or *ARC*. This is the amount of money that actuaries have calculated should be contributed to the pension fund this year. A city will have met its ARC if it contributes that amount to the pension fund this year. The accounting for OPEB funds works essentially the same way as for pension funding, so you'll see the same terms used in discussing OPEB payments.

From a banker's perspective, the important point about pension funding is that the current rules require governments to build up very large pools of investable funds, and invest them, hoping to fund the pensions with the returns. Pension funds are large, and they have an unusual amount of latitude for investing, and that makes them low-hanging fruit to a banker—for better and frequently worse.

# Government banking

The banking services a government uses are not so very different from the services you use, though there are some twists. The most significant twist is that the balances in government bank accounts are typically much larger than the FDIC insurance limits. To insure against loss, governments often demand (well, law usually requires them to demand) that the bank in which they deposit their funds put up collateral for all or part of the deposits. A bank that accepts a million-dollar deposit has to put up a million dollars in T-bills. If the bank happens to have that much in inventory, great. If not, then they have to go get it, substantially

---

[99]The US Postal Service is being driven into bankruptcy by congressional actions that force them to fund their pensions 75 years into the future. This is to say that the Postal Service is losing money today in order to fund retirement benefits for mail carriers who haven't been born yet.

increasing the cost of these funds. This is why it's mostly only the big banks who really want government deposits: they're the only ones with enough collateral just lying around. Smaller banks might seek government deposits only when they want to shore up their capital position (the collateral, being very liquid by definition, looks good to regulators on a bank's books) or are looking for fee income.

Banks also have a program called *CDARS*, which is a way to share large deposits so that each deposit is under the FDIC limits. The National Bank of Dover will accept a $500,000 deposit from the town of Dover and the the National Bank of Foxcroft will accept a $500,000 deposit from the town of Foxcroft. Both will then take $250,000 and deposit it on account at the other's bank. Result: each bank has two fully-insured $250,000 deposits instead of one half-insured $500,000 deposit. The exchange is invisible to the customers, so from each town's perspective, they have a $500,000 account at their local bank. The FDIC's deposit insurance is premium-based, so—in theory—this does not increase the risk to the FDIC's insurance fund.[100]

Another difference between you and your local government is in the accountability. A lot of government money comes with audit requirements. A school department has to be able to show that special education money from the federal government was spent on special education and subsidies for school lunches were spent on school lunches. Frequently, the simplest way to do this is to establish separate bank accounts for each of these funds.[101] Furthermore, some funds are under the control of the personnel department, and some are under the control of the cafeteria. You don't want a low balance in the cafeteria funds to cause paychecks to bounce, so funds with separate lines of authority are often given separate bank accounts. The result of these requirements is that even a small government can manage dozens of different checking accounts.

In addition to these, a government will have interest-bearing accounts for longer-term funds, and the bank will usually offer a convenient way to move money from these accounts into in-

---

[100]CDARS is a private business and, as the name suggests, was originally only about brokered CDs. They have recently expanded to include demand deposits, but for larger governments with millions of dollars flowing in and out each day, this is probably not yet a good solution.

[101]This is hardly the best way to do it, but it is far from uncommon.

vestment accounts, where they can be put into (hopefully) higher-earning money-market funds or something similar. Most governments have a *cash manager*, whose job it is to move money back and forth between the zero-interest checking accounts and investment accounts that earn money, with the goal of making sure the checking accounts are always full, but never too full. As the government gets larger, this job gets substantially more complex. Some banks offer a *zero-balance account* which "pulls" money into a checking account from a companion money-market or investment account as needed to maintain a balance of zero in between check payments.

For security and audit purposes, governments will frequently use payment services like a lockbox, or positive pay. See "Payments" on page 75 for more about those. Managing deposit accounts are the banking basics, but there are plenty more services a bank can provide its government customers, for better and worse.

# Bonds and other borrowing

A government's finances are usually quite circumscribed. Tax rates are set for a year, and modifications to the rate are frequently limited by statute or constitution. The vicissitudes of an economy may make tax revenue rise and fall, but the changes are rarely dramatic. If a government needs to make some investment, building a new road or bridge, for example, it may need a way to amortize that cost over several years. In addition, many governments depend on short-term borrowing—sometimes called a *tax anticipation note (TAN)*—to cover cash flow shortfalls.[102] Borrowing is therefore an essential part of government finance, and since much government borrowing is far beyond the capacity of any individual bank, governments rely on the bond market, a huge source of funds.

The bond market is endlessly complicated, but the basic principles are straightforward. A bond is a legal documentation of a

---

[102]In a way, this is simply saying that in a climate of low interest rates, you can lower taxes simply by keeping less cash in reserve. When cash runs low, you issue a TAN, and life is good again. This seems all well and good, but interest rates won't stay low forever, and rebuilding those cash reserves in a climate of higher interest rates will be very painful when it becomes necessary.

debt, and the market for bonds involves trading pieces of some debt. That's all. Like most debt, there is an interest rate explicit or implicit in the transaction. For example, the city of Sunnydale might sell you a one-year bond for $1000. They are the *issuer* of this bond. The owner of this bond will be entitled to have $1000 from Sunnydale one year from now. You might decide that Sunnydale's promise is not worth much, so you might offer to buy that bond for $909. This much, invested for a year at 10% interest, will amount to $1000, so this is an implicit interest rate of 10%. I, on the other hand, might feel more confident in Sunnydale's promise, so might bid $952, an interest rate of a bit more than 5%. This kind of a bond, where nothing is paid to the bondholder until the bond matures, is called a *zero-coupon bond*. The fact that two people could disagree about how much it's worth provides the basis for a market, and the bond market is just the collection of all the people who buy and sell promises like this to each other.

Another kind of debt is a *coupon bond*, where a city might promise you a stream of interest payments on some borrowed amount, with the principal repaid at the end. For example, Sunnydale might promise a two-year bond of $1000, at 5%. This would commit them to paying $25 to the bondholders every six months for two years, and to pay off the principal value of $1000 at the very end. This bond's *face value*, also called the *par value*, is $1000, and its *coupon rate* is 5%.[103]

At a bond auction, I might agree with Sunnydale that the bond is worth $1000 and pay that much for it, and enjoy a 5% interest rate on my $1000 investment. You, being more skeptical about Sunnydale's ability to repay it, might only bid $800. If there are few enough buyers that you get to buy at that price, you'll still get the same coupon payments as I do, but since your investment was smaller, you get what amounts to a higher interest rate. The *coupon rate* will be the same, but the *yield* will be higher for you.

The exact calculation of the bond yield (also called the *yield to maturity*) is pretty complicated, not least because many bonds have a *call provision* to allow the issuer to pay them off ahead of time. As shorthand, bond traders will refer to the *current yield*, which is just the annual amount returned by the coupons divided by the bond price. In this case, it would be 6.25%.

---

[103]The name is due to the fact that bonds like these were once printed with coupons that could be clipped off the bond and presented for payment.

This is the basic structure, and within it, there are endless variations. A bond is just a contract between two parties, so it can be as varied as any two parties choose to make it. The term can vary, the payments, the call provisions, if any. There can be legal restrictions on what the issuer can do with the money, or how they conduct their business, restrictions on their credit rating, whatever the issuer and underwriter agree will make the bonds easier to sell at a good rate. Most state and local government-issued bonds (called *municipal bonds* even for state-issued notes) are not taxed in the US, but some are, if the IRS deems the purpose to be not 100% public. There exist entire buildings full of lawyers and accountants who work to elaborate these basic concepts, and to adapt them to the needs of any individual issuer and project.[104] The big underwriters find it easier to sell bonds to their buyers if they assert a certain level of uniformity, but there are very few hard and fast rules.

## Selling a bond

After you've worried about the technical details, the other important part of the bond market is finding the buyers, which is the job of an *underwriter*. This is typically an investment bank or team of banks who buys the entire bond issue from the issuer, and sells it to others, presumably making their profit along the way. The underwriter assumes (or is supposed to assume) the risk of marketing the bond issue. The underwriter sells the bond to some collection of bond dealers and institutional investors, who go off and resell them and so on. There is no bond exchange or central location where this is done, it's all pretty ad hoc, with dealers trading with each other through their own, independently developed, networks of customers and other dealers.[105]

---

[104]The enterprising reader who wants to learn more about bonds could do worse than to spend some time clicking around at emma.msrb.org, where thousands of bond disclosure statements are archived, along with prices and yields. This is also as good a time as any to point out that the *CUSIP number* you'll see listed for each bond on the web site is a serial number, assigned by the American Banker's Association, that uniquely identifies any security sold in the US. You can use this number to look it up on Emma or to find a price for it.

[105]One of the things you'll learn from perusing bond documents is that it's nearly impossible to figure out how much the underwriter makes from a bond sale. The profit to them is usually built into the sales, but the prices are the result of an auction, so it is very hard to come up with documentation.

A couple more bits of jargon to equip you. When you sell a bond or some other security to a dealer, you sell it at their quoted *bid price*. This is the price they bid for that security. You will buy a bond from a dealer at the *ask price*, the price they ask from you. Bond prices are often quoted as bid/ask prices, so you might see a price at 99 bid/100 ask. The *spread* is just the difference between the bid and the ask. The spread is a good measure of a bond's liquidity. The narrower the spread, the easier it is for a dealer to resell the bond. Spreads range from half a percent to four percent or more.

One special kind of dealer is called a *market maker*. This is a dealer, usually an investment bank, who publicly commits to always buying some security. They don't guarantee the bid price, but they commit to bidding *something* so that other customers can buy without fear of being stuck with something they can't sell later on. They don't do this in order to be nice, but in order to sell the bonds in the first place. It's a marketing move.

There is also a bond *trustee*, the party charged with actually doing what needs to be done in order to fulfill the transaction. In the Sunnydale example above, someone has to collect the payments from Sunnydale and distribute them to the bondholders, and this is the job of the trustee. If there were some other terms in the bond documents, an escrow fund to establish, for example, or inspections of the bridge to be built, the trustee is responsible for those.

There are several important roles to play in making a bond transaction happen. For any bond issue, there is the *bond counsel*, representing the issuer, who is supposed to review the legality of the whole thing. Working with the *underwriter's counsel*, they come up up with the legal language to require repayment of the loan and whatever conditions they think will help sell the bonds, and put it in a document called the bond *debenture*. This step frequently involves an assortment of other attorneys who might be required for this or that obtuse purpose. There is usually also a *financial advisor* helping a city or county navigate the process. Paying all these lawyers and bankers can be a substantial burden, and that's why a municipality doesn't issue bonds every day.

One consequence of the expense of bond sales is that managing bond proceeds becomes a significant task. A bridge that is going to take three years to build might be financed with a single bond sale, but the funds have to be put somewhere after the sale and before they are spent. IRS rules decree that the bond proceeds can't earn more interest than the coupon rate of the bond if it is is to remain tax-free, so the bond proceeds typically wind up in a set of laddered CDs or some other investments meant to mature at appropriate points during the construction project.

## Varieties of bonds

A bond is just a contract between borrower and lender. Within some fairly broad legal boundaries, a contract can be written however the parties please. Consequently, there is an endless variety of deals into which a city, county, or state government can enter, with an equally endless variety of bonds that might be involved in them. However, the kinds of long-term bonds a government sells usually fall into one of a few broad categories.

**General obligation bond** A bond issued by a government and backed only by their promise to repay it is called a *general obligation bond*. It will receive the credit rating of the government that issued it. For example, the city of Sunnydale might sell a bond to provide the capital with which to build a bridge. After the bridge is built, the city of Sunnydale itself owes the money back to the investors and the payments will come from Sunnydale's tax collections.

**Revenue bond** Suppose the bridge is to be paid for with tolls. Sunnydale might sell the bond as a *revenue bond* instead. In this case, the tolls are the source of repayment for the bond, and not any other tax revenue. Sunnydale is still ultimately responsible for the bonds, but the bond rating will depend both on Sunnydale's bond rating and an assessment of the amount and reliability of the revenue.

**Third-party bond** Suppose Sunnydale wants to borrow to build a new sewer system, and proposes to repay the bond with sewer fees collected by an independent sewer authority. This is a little trickier since the sewer authority is somewhat independent of the main city government. Sunnydale issues the bond, but makes sure that the debenture documents specify that the repayment comes from the sewer revenues, and not from Sunnydale's tax revenues. For this

bond, the rating agencies would look into the sewer authority's finances and the reliability of the sewer fee collection
system and that sort of thing.[106]

**Tax increment financing**  A relatively recent twist on a revenue
bond is a *tax increment financing* (TIF) bond. Sort of a cross
between a general obligation bond and a revenue bond, the
idea is that the revenue stream to repay the bond is supposed to come from the new tax revenue produced by the
project for which the TIF financing is dedicated. For example, Sunnydale might borrow to build a trolley line, on the
theory that the increased construction and property values
along the line will increase the tax revenue to the city and
thus repay the bond. TIF bonds can be a good idea and they
can be a terrible idea. The devil is in the details, especially
including exactly who is on the hook if the revenue is not
adequate to service the debt.[107]

In addition to these, you'll occasionally see reference to *refunding* a bond issue, or a *refunding bond*. "Refunding" is bond-speak
for "refinancing." Since many bond contracts do not allow the
possibility of paying them off early, the process usually involves
buying Treasury bonds and parking them with a trustee so that the
interest and principal of the Treasury bonds will pay off the interest and principal of the original bond issue. The mechanics are a
bit complicated, but you can treat them like a garden-variety refinancing. The concept is the same. A municipality will consider refunding some bonds when the available interest rate falls enough,
or to pay off some debt in the event of a windfall, and so on.

---

[106]If the sewer authority threatens default, you'll hear people say the city has
a *moral obligation* to repay the authority's bond, lest the default damage the city's
own bond rating. Presumably these are people who are frightened of shadows, but
the concern is real and related to the essential caprice of the rating agencies. They
won't flex their muscles in front of a Goldman Sachs or AIG, but they are happy to
bully a city or state by lowering its bond rating.

[107]TIFs are often proposed in conjunction with a commercial project, like a mall
or office park, where they might pay for traffic improvements or utility routing,
making sure that new revenue paid by some commercial developer goes not the
public good, but to benefit the developer. This is not always the case, but it is often
enough they should be approached with skepticism.

## Bond prices

A bond's price is a dollar figure, though the yield is the really important number. A high price means a low yield, or a low effective interest rate. Bond prices will vary for several different reasons, but they boil down to two basic causes: either the investors' fear of being repaid changes, or the interest rate climate changes.

Fear is a challenging emotion to quantify, but financiers have done it, and they do it by getting a *bond rating* from a *credit rating agency*. In the US, there are three big rating agencies, Standard & Poor's, Moody's, and Fitch. These are private corporations, but are so important to the functioning of the US economy that their existence, and the ratings they issue, are incorporated into all kinds of state and federal laws and regulations.[108] The rating agencies issue ratings amounting to credit scores for bond issues, and for bond issuers. These are letter-grades, like AAA or A1. Each agency has its own scale, and they are only partly compatible.

A high rating for an issuer will mean a high price (low interest rate) for its bonds. If a city's bond rating is reduced partway through repayment of some bond, some investors who hold it will sell the bond at a loss to other investors who can accommodate the higher risk. Because they get the bond at a lower price, they'll also see a higher yield. Some bond debentures will contain clauses penalizing the city, too.

Another reason a bond's price can change is a change in the general level of interest rates. Consider a bond sold with a coupon rate of 5%. Presumably this rate incorporates an evaluation of investor risk and the bond's term. Say the bond has an AA rating and a 10-year term. This is a lovely thing, but only until the day that bond investors can buy a different AA bond with a 10-year term that pays 6%. At that point, the first bond will be worth less than its face value, and bond dealers and buyers will look to

---

[108]Sadly, these agencies are also thoroughly compromised. Their business benefits the bond buyers, but they are paid by the sellers, who can (and do) game the agencies to get better ratings for their bonds. In recent years, they have underrated municipal bond issues, costing states and cities billions of dollars, and overrated mortgage bonds, costing the world's economy trillions of dollars. This is a sad state of affairs, but astonishingly there is as yet no widely acceptable substitute. They will be used until an alternative comes along, though Dodd-Frank requires federal agencies to begin to find ways to get references to them written out of existing regulations.

their spreadsheets to figure out what price to buy it that will yield 6%. This is why bonds held as collateral typically have fairly short terms

There are a few different ways for an issuer to borrow another's bond rating to get a better rate in the bond market. An issuer can pay a bank to issue a letter of credit, a guarantee that the bank will pay the bond in the event of default. This bond will get the bank's bond rating. An issuer can also buy *bond insurance*, which is pretty much the same thing, but offered by an insurance company instead of a bank.

A would-be issuer can also access the bond market through another entity. The FHLB sells bonds to investors, and lends the resulting funds to member banks, giving banks access to these funds who are otherwise much too small to have access to this market. Several states have established a *municipal bond bank* to borrow in the bond market on behalf of small towns, and many states and counties have other agencies designed to do the same thing for some special purpose, like infrastructure construction or pollution cleanup.

## Subdividing bonds

The bond market has, traditionally, been the stodgy older brother of the financial markets. It is where investors go who want solid dependable income, as opposed to the flightier stock market and the wacky commodities markets. Short-term notes, whether T-bills or commercial paper, have long been considered a reliable store of money, and longer-term bonds are supposed to be an equally reliable source of income. In consequence, over the years, a number of large bond investors have developed who will only invest in top-quality, AAA-rated, bonds. Some funds, including some pension funds and municipal investment pools, for example, are even legally proscribed from investing in bonds of a lower rating. The result is that, though the bond market is a very large source of money, quite a lot of it is only interested in the top of the credit-rating heap. The top credit-ratings are the ones who pay the least in interest. Marketing a lower-rated bond, therefore, can be a challenge.

One way that banks address these issues is by dividing bonds backed by a set of loans into one or more *tranche*. The way this works is best shown by an example. A mortgage bond represents a share of the income from a set of mortgage loans. For some particular set of such loans, there might be language in the bond documents that award some subset of the bonds first dibs on any income from the loans. This is the "senior" tranche, who gets paid before any other bondholders. The bank sells 90% of the bonds as part of this senior tranche and can essentially guarantee a low, but secure interest rate because they get the first cut of the income. The remaining 10%, they call "junior" and it gets whatever interest income is left over (if any). If you expect $100 million of mortgages to return $4 million per year in income, you might write the bond so that 90% of the bonds share the first $2 million of income. This is about a 2.2% interest rate (2/90), low but (theoretically) secure because more than half the loans have to default before the total interest collected is less than $2 million. The security gets a high bond rating, so the bank can find investors to buy it. The remaining 10% of the shares gets the *second* 50% of the income, and assumes the first 50% of any losses. This income is affected if *any* of the loans don't perform, so it's riskier, but it also gets a much higher payoff, as much as 20% (2/10) if no one defaults.

The banks were able to get the ratings agencies to rate the senior tranches of these bonds "AAA," allowing a wide variety of institutional investors to buy them. And since the interest rates these bonds paid is pretty much whatever the bank wants to write into their bond documents, they could set the rate to just slightly higher than any other competing AAA investment, making them very attractive investments to the managers of these institutional funds.

In practice, these tranche arrangements became utterly baroque in their complexity, with several more tiers of risk and banks selling bonds whose tranches were backed by collections of tranches of other bonds, and far worse. But the basic idea remains the same: some of the buyers get security in exchange for a lower return while others get more risk and presumably a better return. Of course, none of the assumptions about risk made to create these tranches held true in 2007 and 2008, when a tidal wave of foreclosures overwhelmed all the risk models.

The other catch is the one that sank Lehman Brothers. If you divide your bonds into high-risk and low-risk tranches, it's easy to sell the low-risk parts, but to whom do you sell the high-risk? Even if it earns a good rate, the buyer might lose the whole investment. Whether by choice, or by necessity, Lehman kept a lot of the high-risk tranches of bonds they constructed on their books, and losses from that were more than enough to overwhelm their capital. They were packaging risk to make it easy to pass it along, but they didn't, or couldn't, pass it all. Doubtless a lot of their customers were grateful for that in the end.

If they couldn't find buyers for the high-risk tranches, why didn't they stop making them? After all, those tranches were the byproduct of financial products engineered by Lehman itself. Presumably they could have stopped sometime before they ran aground on these shoals. Amid the wreckage of a company, it's always difficult to find answers to questions like this, since everyone has an incentive to blame someone else. The aerial view tells us that, apart from the question of individuals' incentives, the firm's biggest source of income was the fees and profits from creating those mortgage bonds, including the toxic tranches. It would have taken a strong leader to shut that down, something that was apparently lacking at the time.

# Predatory public finance

> Timeo danistas et donas ferentes.
>
> > *"I fear money lenders bearing gifts."* Not
> > *from Virgil's Aeneid, which had Laocoön*
> > *fearing Greeks bearing gift horses.*

It's a sad fact that a description of the relationship between banks and governments can't be considered complete without an examination of the many ways in which the current landscape of the banking industry is a veritable minefield for taxpayers. Governments need banks, and bankers know it—and frequently use the fact to their advantage. This, of course, is no different than any other supplier of services to a government—school districts need teachers, and teachers know it, too—until it goes over the line, past what used to be the bounds of propriety. In the case of Philadelphia's interest rate swaps, the abrupt decline in interest rates made what had seemed a prudent hedge into a phenomenally profitable deal.[109]

---

[109] "A deal's a deal," they say, but where is the line between profit and exploitation? Imagine a wealthy banker offering his neighbor some money for his cabin

Financial transactions involving a government are often large
and complex. A bond sale can involve a small legion of bankers
and lawyers, and take several steps to be executed. This provides
a multitude of nooks and crannies into which fees and profit can
be tucked, especially where there is no tradition of fiduciary responsibility of the banker to his or her customer. There are also
many transactions whose purpose involves the transfer of risk
from a bank to a customer. Usually for a fee, of course, but risk is
hard to quantify and hard to communicate effectively, even when
one wants to. Far too often, our governments have been the vic-
tims of these transactions, not the beneficiaries.

Here, then, is another short and incomplete list, containing
some of the ways in which banks have recently profited in un-
seemly fashion from their government customers.

**Swaption** Philadelphia's interest-rate swap was bad enough, but
in 2004, Northampton County, a rural county in eastern
Pennsylvania's Lehigh Valley, sold an interest rate *swaption* to Merrill Lynch (now BankAmerica). A swaption is a
promise to enter into an interest rate swap, and in this case,
Merrill Lynch paid the county about $1.9 million up front
(less $300,000 in fees) for the right to swap fixed for float-
ing interest rates in 2012. By 2012, it was clear this was a
really bad idea, but terminating the agreement on the eve
of the swap invoked penalty clauses that cost the county
$27 million.[110]

**Bond churning** In 2005, the state of Louisiana sold $650 million
of bonds to refinance existing debt at a lower interest rate.
About $45 million of that debt had only been issued three
months earlier, in October, at more or less the same interest rate. Citigroup, the underwriter of the earlier bond, and
one of the underwriters of the bigger sale, essentially sold
the same bond twice, earning $665,000 in fees for the first

---

on a cruise because it's a little closer to the lifeboats. That's paying to hedge some
risk. He's happy; the neighbor's happy. There's a mutual benefit: the banker has
reduced his risk, the neighbor has a little extra money. Now imagine the ship has
sunk, the neighbor is in the water, swimming towards the lifeboat the banker is in.
The neighbor begs for the life jacket the banker is wearing. Is this part of the deal
that must be honored? Does the banker have a right to refuse to give it up?

[110]McCalls, Samantha Marcus, May 22, 2012, tinyurl.com/checkingthebanks-
swaption (no hyphen).

sale, and $104,000 in fees for refinancing just those October bonds.[111]

**Letters of credit** Municipal bond borrowers frequently use a letter of credit from a bank to prop up their own bond rating and lower the interest to be paid on a bond. Essentially the bank is offering a guarantee for the bond, and so its bond rating becomes more material than the municipality or agency issuing the bond. The problem is that letters of credit expire, typically in three or four years, while a bond might not be paid off for 30 years. When the letter of credit expires, the municipality must get another, or be forced to pay the bond back immediately. Unfortunately, with the demise of several large banks in the 2008 crisis, letters of credit are harder to come by now, and the fees banks charge for them have risen dramatically. In 2010, the Port of Oakland saw a $2 million increase in their LOC fees to back up a $200 million line of credit using the commercial paper market.[112]

**Pension obligation bonds** The idea with a pension obligation bond is to borrow at a low rate, put the resulting money into the pension funds, and convert a 7.5–8.5% debt to the pension fund to address the unfunded liability into a 5–6% debt, more what a municipality might expect to pay on a taxable bond. This might sound like a great idea, but in the end it's just gambling, since the 7.5–8.5% target on pension investments is the discount rate for the obligations, which is ever so slightly different from the expected rate of return. (See "Pension funds" on page 125.) That is, everyone fondly hopes the pension fund managers will meet that target, and the evidence is that they do a decent job of it on average, but there is no guarantee. In 2008, Connecticut borrowed $2.28 billion to top up its teachers retirement fund. That was the moment the stock market, in which most of those funds were invested, tanked. When the bond was issued in April, the Dow Jones average stood at 13,000, and by the following November, it was just over 6,600. At this point, in 2013, the

---

[111]Bloomberg news, Darrell Preston, February 24, 2005, archived at tinyurl.com/checkingthebankschurning.

[112]These numbers are from the Port of Oakland's annual reports and agenda minutes. On the brighter side, in 2012, with competition in the LOC market somewhat restored, Oakland's LOC fees came down somewhat.

investments may have almost returned to near their original value, but Connecticut has been paying 5.88% interest in the meantime, along with ample fees to the banks that underwrote the bonds in the first place. There are years left on the terms to those bonds, so there is time to catch up, but the risks remain immense.[113]

**Capital appreciation bonds**  A capital appreciation bond is sort of like a zero-coupon bond, but instead of being sold at a discount from the face value, the bond is sold as returning a fixed rate of interest. In both cases, the value of the bond plus all the accrued interest is paid in one lump at the end. From a government's point of view, the important distinction is that the face value of the bond is the discounted number, so if you're worried about the total debt of your town, this can make it look smaller. For example, you might sell a $1,000 zero-coupon bond with a ten-year term for $558 to someone who bids a 6% interest rate. The bond will count as a $1,000 debt in the municipality's accounting. A capital appreciation bond of the same amount would count as a $558 debt in the accounting.[114] It's a great way for a mayor to hide how much debt has been taken on, that doesn't sound completely terrible until you do the math. Unfortunately, the unpaid interest compounds, essentially becoming part of the principal, so the costs add up quickly. Starting at $558, and making ten years of semi-annual interest payments at 6% (the way a coupon bond would work) would cost $750 total. This would include only $192 in interest, less than half the $442 of the capital appreciation bond

For a longer term, it's quite easy for the interest to exceed the principal by a lot. In 2011, the Poway Unified School District which serves the city of Poway, California, and part of San Diego, borrowed $105 million on a 40-year capital appreciation bond. They will make some interest payments starting around the year 2031, but otherwise no payments are due until maturity, in 2051. When the bond is done, they'll have

---

[113]Connecticut treasurer's office reports, and tinyurl.com/checkingthebankspob.

[114]The math is precisely the same, but somehow relabeling it makes a difference to accountants, go figure.

repaid the principal and $877 million in interest, *eight times* the principal.[115]

**Bond flipping** There is a conflict in incentives in the bond underwriting business. The issuer of the bond wants as low an interest rate as possible (as high a price as possible at the initial bond sale), but the underwriter wants to stay friends with its big institutional clients, who want to purchase the bonds as cheaply as possible. And a big part of the reason they want them cheap is to resell them. If a bond dealer or big institutional investor can buy a bunch of newly-issued bonds from some city at 5% and then turn around and sell them at 4.5%, he has made a tidy profit, but he's also proven that there are people who would have bought them from the city at 4.5%. The higher interest rate is money paid by taxpayers, not going to a public purpose, but only to make a profit for the underwriter's friends. Banks have been accused of giving preference to certain dealers during bond sales, filling their orders at low prices while there are still other orders unfilled. The SEC and FINRA have discussed new rules to prevent this in the past couple of years, but the obscurity of the bond sale process has prevented any real oversight.[116]

**Padding bond sales** It is very difficult to get more than a vague picture of the underwriting profit earned from an issuer for any specific bond transaction. The bond prospectus is supposed to answer such questions, and some of the fees may be outlined, but to understand the amount earned usually requires understanding the whole transaction. This makes it relatively easy for banks to include costs that have nothing to do with the bond. In December 2012, FINRA fined five banks $3.3 million for padding the fees they collected from bond sales with dues they paid to Cal PSA, a California lobbying association. The banks, including Citigroup, Goldman Sachs, JPMorgan, Merrill Lynch (BankAmerica), and Morgan Stanley, were also forced to pay $1.13 million in

[115]Voice of San Diego, Will Carless, August 6, 2012, tinyurl.com/checkingthebankspoway.

[116]Business Insider, Vincent Fernando, August 11, 2009, tinyurl.com/checkingthebanksflipping.

restitution to a number of municipal and state issuers in California.[117] Cal PSA was billing its members according to the volume of bonds they underwrote, so apparently members found it easy just to tack the bills onto their underwriting fees.

**Tax Anticipation Notes** Tax revenues have an ebb and a flow each year. Income taxes tend to bump in April, despite the withholding rules, and sales tax collections bump in December and January after the Christmas shopping binge. A government that depends on income taxes might find itself short in March, and can sell a tax anticipation note (TAN) to get through the month until the April tax returns start rolling in. (You'll also see them as *revenue anticipation note.*) In an earlier, more innocent time, the chance of a shortfall would be the reason a government would maintain a cash reserve. This reserve would be idle most of the year, when it could be invested in T-bills, and only used for a short time. A government that relies on TANs not only gives up that investment income, but also pays all the bond issuance costs each year. San Diego pays about $200,000 each year on the TAN issuance fees alone. This year, they expect to pay $300,000 more in interest, though that is thankfully down from $5 million in 2008.[118]

**LIBOR rigging** The London interbank interest rate (*LIBOR*) is a benchmark interest rate, to which millions of other interest rates in hundreds of *trillions* in investments refer. When a group of banks admitted to rigging LIBOR in 2012, they were essentially admitting to having stolen money from the parties involved in these agreements. Some $200 billion of municipal interest rate swaps sold before the 2008 crisis were tied to LIBOR, and rigging the rate made the swaps themselves more expensive and getting out of them more expensive, too. Bloomberg news estimated that the additional costs to municipalities exceeds $6 billion.[119]

---

[117]FINRA decision: tinyurl.com/checkingthebankspadding.

[118]San Diego annual financial reports.

[119]Bloomberg News, Darrell Preston, October 9, 2012 tinyurl.com/checkingthebankslibor.

In addition to all these, there are the more pedestrian sorts of fees, the sort that plague any modern bank customer. Because many government bank accounts have very high traffic, the fee income can be quite substantial. Furthermore, because a city or county government can be quite complicated, it is usually a major undertaking to change banks. A government thus has very little leverage in the banking market.

Again, the purpose behind enumerating these different forms of bad behavior is not to revel in the villainy of some bankers, but to be specific about the problems that need solving. Governments entered many of these deals because they felt they were going to get something useful out of them—some extra income from the interest-rate swaps, low (or hidden) payments from the capital appreciation bonds, lower interest rates from the letters of credit, the ability to spend their cash reserve on something else, and so on. Understanding what governments truly need is an important step in designing institutions to serve those needs, and understanding the specifics of bank excesses is an important step in designing regulations and laws to prevent those abuses in the future.

What's remarkable about the conduct on display here is not simply the lack of consideration for schoolchildren, taxpayers, and so on, but that many governments, if not most, *have* the assets they need to conduct their own financial business. Our governments' ends could be handled with their own means. Unfortunately, the wealth controlled by those governments is seldom organized in such a way that they can do so easily, if at all.

For example, the state of Rhode Island, with an approximately $7 billion annual budget, has around a half-billion dollars in investments on hand at any one time and three times that amount in cash and bank balances, scattered around the state government.[120] But with over $2 billion on hand, so little of it is available to invest that the state had to borrow from (sell bonds to) insurance companies like Allstate and State Farm to finance $20 million in drinking water improvements in 2013.[121] Bonds issued to out of state buyers represents interest payments sent beyond the state's borders, lost to the state's economy, and it also represents underwriting fees, bond counsel fees, broker commissions, and on and on. The state paid over $13 million in these fees in 2012, and that's

---

[120]This does *not* count the $7.3 billion in the state's pension fund.
[121]This was only one of several bonds issued that year.

not counting costs built into the proceeds of the bond sales. This represented about 4% of the total funds borrowed that year.

Numbers as large as this can seem too abstract. Let's scale it down a bit. Imagine you're rich enough to have $2 million in your checking and savings accounts, but your accountant has arranged your finances so that you need to take out a car loan to buy a $20,000 car. And then imagine you have to pay 4 points ($800) in loan fees, on top of the interest you'll pay. Would you put up with that? Would you not find a new accountant?

Those considering the creation of alternative financial institutions can think of the above list as a collection of potential business opportunities for those new institutions. Here is demand, these examples say; is there a more seemly way to meet it? (Others can simply marvel at the variety and the ingenuity on display.)

Some of this work is already underway. For example, in 2012, the Build America Mutual bond insurance company was formed to insure municipal bonds. It is a mutual insurance company, so is owned by the municipalities whose bonds it insures. It is also brand-new, so whether it can maintain a level of service and accountability better than its for-profit competitors is an open question, presumably to be answered over the next few years.[122]

Other small reforms are also feasible. Simply creating a legal requirement that banks act in a fiduciary capacity for one's customers would go a long way. For example, in Vermont, mortgage brokers can be legally liable if a loan goes bad due to fraud or inadequate disclosure. Consequently, Vermont saw virtually no increase in foreclosures before or during the 2008 crisis, while the rest of the country was inundated.

It is crystal clear that in many ways, banks regard our state and local governments as marks to whom they can sell the newest, shiniest, financial gimmick, no matter how risky or rigged. Really, though, if a bank is paying you to take some risk they don't want to take, there is a warning hiding in there, and not too deep. The good news about this is that state and local governments can be fairly accessible places, and even occasionally responsive to public pressure. Our cities, towns, counties, and states have the financial wherewithal to avoid being preyed upon, but it seems we need to force them to act that way.

---

[122]See buildamerica.com.

## *Seven*

# Potential banking scenarios

AMONG OTHER THINGS, the financial crisis of 2008 was a striking illustration of how destructive the financial system has become to the real economy. Large swaths of the US economy were laid waste, partly due to the hubris and greed of the people in control of the nation's most important financial institutions, but also due to the system of incentives they have constructed to run those institutions.

In the search for new financial institutions to supplant the ones we have now, some of the following ideas may prove useful. As presented, almost none of them will work, due to differences in local laws and economic conditions. But they are not far off from ideas that *will* work, so are here in the hopes that they will illustrate the range of ideas possible, as well as provide a certain amount of pump-priming to the reader's imagination. What do you think might be possible?

## Mutual banks and credit unions

The last 30 years of banking history have seemed to pass by two very useful institutions: credit unions and mutual banks. This is a shame since, in many ways, these two species of bank embody a more equitable and useful future for finance. Both are essentially co-operatives in nature, owned by their depositors. They are in some sense, very democratic institutions, despite not having anything to do with the government. (Or at least they can be.)

A *credit union* is typically organized around some community of interest: a workplace, a union, a neighborhood. They typically need at least a couple thousand members to be viable, so

the community can't be too small. They are a co-operative structure, with the credit union ownership resting with the depositors.
Put money into a *share account* and you're an owner, not just a
member.

Credit unions used to be limited to car loans and small consumer lending. Though they are still more or less limited to
serving consumer banking needs, the range of services they provide is much wider, ranging from real estate lending to credit or
debit cards. In some circumstances they can make small business
loans, too.

One of the other good things about credit unions is that a vast
number of them are started by non-bankers. This means that the
National Credit Union Administration (the FDIC of credit unions)
has plenty of experience with inexperience. Which is why their
web site (www.ncua.gov) has a great deal of useful information
about how to go about starting and running a credit union, and
it's all aimed at novices.

There are a couple of catches to a credit union. One is that
for the most part, a credit union's only way to grow is through
retained earnings. Their capital is made up of a subsection of
their deposit accounts (the share accounts), along with retained
earnings. They have no stock to sell, so there is a limit to how
quickly they can grow, and enforces a quite conservative outlook.
It also introduces a certain amount of balance sheet risk to their
operation, and can force them into situations where they have
more leverage than they are comfortable with. They will sometimes actually need to discourage deposits because they don't
have enough capital to maintain their regulatory ratios, either by
turning customers away or, more usually, by lowering the interest
rates they pay.[123]

A *mutual bank* is sort of like a credit union, with a somewhat
broader mandate. A mutual bank is freer to make business loans,
for example, and there are other services open to them. The OCC
would be the regulator for most mutual banks. A mutual bank's
capital is made up of *pledged deposits*. These are deposits commit-
ted for a matter of years. They typically don't earn interest, but the
bank's earnings can be paid as dividends to the owners of those

---

[123]Under federal credit union regulations, there is a category of "low-income
credit union" that can accept non-member deposits and "secondary capital" accounts to shore up a credit union's capital position.

deposits.[124] Though they are deposits, and so seem as if they belong among a bank's liabilities, the rules for mutual banks allow them to be counted as capital, like a credit union's share accounts. Mutual banks are an old form of banking. The nation's first savings bank, in Philadelphia, was a mutual bank. They originally tended to cluster at a slight remove from the financial centers. The idea in those days was that the relationship between the bank and the business was the security for a loan, so there was a certain unwillingness of most banks to loan beyond their sphere. Mutual banks were a way for a group of businesses, each of whom needed credit, to pool their resources to help each other out.

In recent years, mutual banks have fallen out of favor. A booster of mutual banks explained it to me this way: "No one gets rich in a mutual bank." Which explains why hundreds of mutual banks were converted to conventional stock banks in the 1980s and 1990s, producing windfalls for a number of well-connected banking executives. Of course, lots of those institutions later went bust, but this is an indictment of the conduct and practice, not the structure.

## Public banks

In the search for alternatives to the existing financial institutions and system we've got, many advocates find inspiration in the example of the Bank of North Dakota (BND), the only real government-owned bank in the United States. A movement has grown up to advocate for the establishment of more banks like it.[125] The public bank movement envisions banking as a kind of utility: essential for the operation of the economy, but a mere aid to sensible economic policy, not the focus of it. The financialization of the economy is not all to the good, for the economy, the government, or the majority of the people who live in it.

This is hardly a stretch. In much of the rest of the world, public banks play a huge role in the advancement of the economy. Germany has a substantial network of regional public banks that

---

[124]This isn't just a semantic game; dividends only happen when the bank makes a profit, while interest is a promise unrelated to the bank's profitability.

[125]See publicbankinginstitute.org for much more information about BND, about efforts to establish state banks around the country, and public banks in general.

make crucial investments in their manufacturing economy. *All* of the Asian economies, whose industrialization has overtaken the US in so many ways, rely heavily on financial institutions run for public purposes rather than private profit. Over the past 30 years, the public financial institutions of China have created the industrial miracle that is the Chinese economy.[126]

Over the same 30 years, the private financial industry in the US has brought us to the brink of financial collapse several times, and facilitated the economic miracle in China by cutting costs at US companies so thoroughly they have to go overseas to "compete." All in service of subjecting US industry to a cost-benefit analysis that completely ignores public factors, like considerations of the quality of life around shuttered factories. Our financial system is impressive in many ways but it defies common sense to think we have nothing to learn from the countries who have eaten our industrial lunch these past few decades.

There are real advantages to looking to state and local government in an effort to reform the financial landscape. First of all, there is a lot of money there. The government of even a small town of 20,000 likely has bank accounts with millions of dollars in them. There are over 30,000 towns, and 3,000 counties in the country, along with the states. Collectively, this is many hundreds of billions of dollars, and with the states is certainly more than a trillion. Second, they are approachable. In a search for accountability, this means a lot.

Finally, public money tends to be quite predictable. A government receives tax bills at legally-prescribed times of year, and the budgeted revenues and expenses are debated in public, so the ebb and flow of its finances tend to be fairly easy to predict. Typically, a bank startup will take a few years to fill out its loan portfolio, as the bank management learns how its customers tend to behave: how much cash they need, what times of year (or month) demand is highest, and so on. A bank that relies heavily on public funds could get up to speed somewhat more quickly, since the important variables are widely known or readily predictable, and some of the sponsoring governments' demand for credit could fill out the loan portfolio soon.

---

[126]Along with the Brobdingnagian environmental disasters that accompany it. These, though, are a consequence of the shortsighted use of a powerful tool, and do not have anything to say about the tool itself.

## Beyond North Dakota

One of the big problems facing public bank advocates is that a public bank hasn't been started in the US in the more than 90 years since the Bank of North Dakota was established. The financial and political world has changed a lot since then. For example, BND was established before the FDIC was, and it never accepted deposit insurance. Its deposits are guaranteed directly by the citizens of North Dakota. This is a workable system, obviously, but will seem very foreign to officials in other states. There are real opportunities for states, counties, and municipalities to improve their economies and their finances through public ownership or control of financial institutions, but they need to be found and refined by activists who are thinking about the difficulties of starting a bank, not just about the benefits of already having one.

What's more, a banking proposal has to serve a currently unmet need that others perceive. Many years have elapsed since BND was founded, and most of what BND does is accomplished in other states, perhaps not as well or as cheaply, but accomplished nonetheless. BND makes economic development loans; so do hundreds of economic development authorities across the country. BND does collaboration loans with local banks; so do lots of revolving funds run by housing authorities and CDCs. BND does North Dakota's cash management; so do most state Treasury Departments. This isn't to say that BND doesn't do them better or cheaper, it just means that advocates can't present those things as evidence that a public bank is fabulous without also explaining why it would do these jobs better than the existing structures. To a legislator it may not be completely obvious why it's an advantage to use tax dollars instead of borrowed dollars to make economic development loans. An advocate who can speak knowledgeably about the cost of funds in the bond market, the machinations of the ratings agencies, and the ways to reduce credit risk to a public bank will likely make more headway than someone who can only talk about the need to democratize finance.

Also, in a climate where government only seems ever to feel the knife, public banking proponents have to make the argument not only to leaders who care about the health of the local economy, but also to bean-counters who care only about the government's own bottom line. For many governments, it won't be enough just to say it will make the local economy stronger. You also have to show stronger finances, or out-and-out savings in the government checkbook.

In some respects, the public banking movement's focus on North Dakota is well-deserved. BND is a great success, and a wonderful example of how adding some democracy to our financial system can result in greater prosperity for everyone. But it's wrong to suggest there are not downsides. Banking is essentially the management of risk, and people's appetite for risk varies, and even more so when you're talking about public funds. It's not completely irrational for legislators to be risk-averse, and public banking does require the assumption of some risk.[127] Also, with great power comes great responsibility, as Spiderman learned. A public bank, like any bank, is well suited to lose a lot of money if it's managed badly. Operational risk is, after all, one of the sources of banking risk.

## More possibilities

A statewide bank on the North Dakota model is not the only possible application of public banking. Here are a few other possibilities, each of which would add some accountability to portions of the financial markets and could save money for governments or redirect capital to important local needs. As is obvious to anyone with eyes to see, governments vary tremendously in their circumstances, their assets, and the quality of their leadership. An ideal solution for one government might be a terrible waste for another, or a terrible risk. But the principle of public banking is sound, if only as a statement about how destructive our current financial system is. Creating more democratic accountability for our financial system helps governments, and the communities they serve.

Following is a random collection of ideas for banking in the public interest. They are only outlines, meant to illustrate what might be possible. To use them, an activist would have to adapt them to the local economic conditions, state laws, and institutions. None of them are as ambitious as the full-blown state bank model,

---

[127]The aversion to risk does, sometimes, create silly scenarios, such as in Rhode Island in 1991, when the state declined to keep open many of 45 credit unions and small banks insured by a private deposit insurance scheme that failed. Keeping the credit unions open with no other insurance would have been risking over a billion dollars, a third of the state's annual budget at the time. In the event, though, political pressure forced the state to pay back all the depositors anyway. In other words, in order to avoid risking a billion dollars, the state paid...a billion dollars.

but they are all ways to help put public dollars safely to work for public purposes, and that is a goal, where a specific structure is just the means.

## Beef up a CDFI

Several years ago, Congress, at the behest of HUD and the Treasury department, created an opportunity for communities to experiment with new forms of financial institution. A *community development financial institution (CDFI)* is not so much a definition as a niche. The idea is that Community Development Corporations (CDCs) and organizations like them often find unmet needs in the financial services landscape in the (generally poor) communities they serve. Across the country, such organizations have created financial services ranging from revolving funds, to microloan efforts, to credit unions. The Treasury, by granting them special recognition, sought to solidify their position and encourage their growth. Accredited CDFIs can, for example, access lines of credit at the Federal Home Loan Banks (FHLB), and have a leg up in HUD grant programs.

What CDFIs seldom have is reliable access to enough capital. (Though some do.) By and large, the CDCs that sponsor them are organizations used to scrounging, and through cobbling together grants, donations, and savings, many of them have achieved the size necessary to make a difference. If a city or state government wanted to provide capital to them at low cost, it could start a small bank expressly designed to do exactly that.

The way this could work is a pension fund or some part of the government that can make long-term un-collateralized investments might put up $10 million as the bank's equity capital, with which it would buy T-bills, or deposit it all at the FHLB. Using that as collateral, the bank could accept $10 million in deposits from another part of the government that needs collateral behind its deposits, but is content to make medium-term investments. The new bank could then provide a series of *laddered investments*[128] amounting to, say, $9.5 million to the CDFI. The CDFI will pay interest, which would accrue mainly to the arm of the government

---

[128]This means a series of long-term commitments arranged so that at any one time, one of them will mature soon. Imagine taking $12,000, and buying a one-year $1,000 CD each month for a year. During the second year, you're never more than a month away from getting $1,000 back, but all $12,000 is invested at a one-year term, normally at higher rates than you could get for one-month terms.

that put up the cash. That arm, that made the original investment, would get shares of the new institution, now worth twice its original $10 million investment.

| Assets: | **$20.0 million** |
| --- | --- |
| Cash, T-bills, collateral | $10.5 million |
| Loans | $9.5 million |
| **Liabilities & Capital** | **$20.0 million** |
| Owed to depositor(s) | $10.0 million |
| Capital | $10.0 million |

This is a paper gain, of course, but funds like pension funds or self-insurance funds often have low liquidity requirements and high demand for return, and over time the paper gain could be realized, though slowly. Depending on the terms of the CDFI lending, it could be made to be relatively straightforward to unwind in an emergency.

Something like this would be relatively low-overhead to run, and would likely require no employees or space. How exactly to do it—how the governance would work—would depend on the banking laws of the state it's done in. There are issues of concentration risk to work out (perhaps the bank invests in several CDFIs, or perhaps the CDFI itself develops a way to spread the risk of investment), but these can be overcome in many states.

## Service bureau

Another model might be to put aside the lending at first, and concentrate on solving an immediate and real problem facing municipalities and states: because of the collateral requirements, it is generally only the largest banks that can afford to offer services to even smallish governments. It takes a substantial bank to be able to put up $5-10 million in collateral to accept a city or town's deposits, and that's a perfectly normal amount of money for a town of even 20,000 people. Those big banks, in turn, tend to care less about the communities they serve than the little banks.[129] So what you have is a situation where it is very difficult for a government

---

[129]Key word being "tend." There are obnoxious small banks out there, you'll be shocked to know. IndyMac, after all, was a thrift, a kind of bank meant to be a community-centric consumer-oriented bank.

to patronize the banks that care most about the community the government serves.

The general pain-in-the-neck quality of municipal customers (lots of small deposits, lots of withdrawals, high demands for security and liquidity) also means that a city that goes to a BankAmerica or Wells Fargo to request better service for its community will get little response. Moving from one bank to another is typically a difficult process for any customer as complicated as a government, so there is little leverage over the bank. Threats to "move our money" will likely be met with an invitation to not let the door hit you on the way out.

However, a large enough city or county, or a collection of small ones, could put together enough deposits to fund a stand-alone co-op that contracts directly with financial industry vendors to manage bank accounts for these municipal customers. Rather than hold the money or lend it themselves, the co-op would simply deposit it in local banks. Since several banks are involved, each local bank would absorb only as much in deposits as they had the appetite (read: collateral) for.

Comparatively, there is almost no capital in this process, so with $75 million on deposit, the balance sheet might look roughly like this:

| Assets: | **$75.5 million** |
| --- | --- |
| Deposits at other banks | $75.0 million |
| Management assets | $0.5 million |
| Liabilities & Capital | **$75.5 million** |
| Owed to depositor(s) | $75.0 million |
| Capital | $0.5 million |

"Management assets" would be the software to run the bank, the agreements with the cooperating banks, the lease on the servers, and so forth.

The advantage here is both that the city could patronize banks that will keep money circulating locally, and that the city now has relationships with several banks instead of just one. It can play them off each other and ask them to bid for its business, or it can be the leader of a cooperative effort and ask them to participate in lending initiatives like citizen energy efficiency or lead abatement programs. It can ask them to collaborate on funding a bond issue, it can ask them to concentrate some lending in the city, or whatever else comes from having several banks around the same table with (more or less) the same goals. The organization also becomes a natural place for shared services, maybe a guarantee fund to enhance business lending, or a way to share financial management services or bonding among several governments.

Furthermore, by becoming a part of the financial network, and with a relationship to financial industry service providers, the co-op could provide services like sending money, or electronic bill pay, to its citizens.

Such an organization, over time, could begin to accumulate some capital. Under the current low yields, it would be hard to earn very much more than the operating costs, but if a way could be found to provide capital, it would be natural to use it as collateral for its deposits, lowering the cost of funds to the participating banks, and increasing the yields they offer.

Alternatively, it's possible that over time, the cash manager running the co-op's investments will become confident that some of the money on deposit could be used for long-term investing, and maybe use that to capitalize a small bank. Either way, the co-op, while not a bank on its own, could easily become a route to a bank.[130]

## Services for the unbanked

Among the real problems faced by communities across the country is the abandonment of the poor by the financial industry. Actually, that's not a completely fair characterization. Conventional banks are indeed scarce in poor neighborhoods across the country. When you do your accounting per-branch, it's pretty obvious that the cost of funds is going to be much higher in a branch in a poor neighborhood than in a rich one. As banks become less excited about branches in general and consumers become less tethered to them, this distinction should matter less and less, and yet it still does.

But the demand for financial services still exists, in neighborhoods rich and poor. People still get paid with checks, and they still need safe places to store money, and they need to borrow.

---

[130]Of course, it could become a route to something else constructive, too. Sometimes you just don't know what's possible until you're all sitting around a table working together on a goal.

Therefore, when conventional banks abandon a place, or a line of business, their place is typically taken by high-fee financial institutions like payday lenders and check-cashing stores. These places will cash a check for a fee, or they'll offer a cash advance on a paycheck at astronomical rates of interest. (Where it's not outlawed by usury laws.) Prepaid debit cards have, in some places, overtaken savings accounts as safe stores of money.

The problem is that these are all quite expensive services, and quite profitable. There is substantial risk in payday lending, but charging a 10% fee for a two-week loan, which is not unusual, is an annual interest rate exceeding 260%. Prepaid debit cards usually charge a fee for money going in and also for money going out, and check cashing can cost a substantial percentage of the check being cashed.[131]

There is plenty of room here for a public entity, or a private entity uninterested in exploiting the poor, to find a way to provide service at far lower cost to individuals, and therefore to the community they serve. An institution established for some other purpose and therefore already a part of the financial network might find it very little trouble to establish a lower-fee debit card, for example. Perhaps it might find an agency with deep community ties, such as a community development corporation or service non-profit through which to offer such service. Providing the means through which a housing shelter could offer low-cost savings or credit services to its clientele might be a useful service addition.

## Alliance of small towns

In many states, the pressure for small towns to consolidate services in order to economize has build substantially over the past several years. Sharing banking services might be an easy way to do just that, with a mutual bank of small governments. As with any public banking idea, finding the capital is a challenge in an environment of constant government cutbacks. However, with enough towns to participate, it would be a relatively small amount for each participant, and the mutual bank has the advantage that

---

[131]On the other hand, banks are not really an option for small and short-term personal loans these days. To a certain extent, payday lenders exist to fill a service void that banks have consciously declined to fill. Efforts to move the "unbanked" to banks will founder absent an understanding of the services that are actually of greatest value to the poor.

the capital remains, in a legal sense, liquid. Managed correctly, it should be possible to let any member out of the association in an emergency, though bank regulators frown on this since bank capital is not supposed to come and go.

A government mutual bank like this could have positive cash flow from the beginning using a foundation of the cities' own debt. In a climate of higher interest rates, you could do this by refunding bond issues to take advantage of lower interest rates available from the cities' own bank. As of 2013, interest rates have been so low for so long that there are very few refunding opportunities (i.e. high-interest debt) left out there. But bonds for impending large construction projects, planned correctly, could provide a base of relatively good yields for such a bank, allowing a bank like this to skip the usual few years of losses for de novo banks, something else that is probably important in conversations with public officials about banking.

Municipal bond issues, though long-term, are also fairly liquid. A seller will take some loss if interest rates rise, but because there is a robust market for these bonds, this kind of debt does not lock in a bank for the entire term of the bond, decreasing the liquidity risk to the bank.

A vehicle like this could also serve as a way for small governments to share services, or to share access to more financial expertise than they have access to. As with all of these ideas, it's worth considering not simply what it could be, but also what it could become.

One of the difficulties with such a plan is the potential disparities among members. A mutual arrangement with a single large member with many small ones is potentially destabilizing since withdrawals the large member might have to make could dwarf the remaining pool of resources. No one wants to be in a pool with a gorilla, and the gorilla isn't so wild about it either. The more members, the less of a problem this becomes, but it is a governance issue that must be addressed early on.

## Assemblage of parts

Given the political and fiscal realities of any particular locale, a real public bank might not be feasible for any number of reasons: political, financial, whatever. But it may well be that the same goal is feasible through interconnected but independent pieces.

For example a service bureau, as described above, isn't a bank, but it looks like one from the outside. Were it to find a CDFI with which to cooperate, you could very well have targeted economic development accomplished by leveraging public funds, without the actual bank at the center of it. This could be a structure that might eventually grow into a bank.

Similarly, a public bond bank established to give a collection of municipalities access to the bond market might find a way to help provide funds to start up a credit union. Bond funds have to be parked somewhere between the sale of the bonds and their use by the municipality involved.[132] If they were put into a credit union CD, that would be a relatively stable (or at least predictable) source of funding that could help immensely during the startup phase to such a project.

Once you have a goal in mind for your banking project, remember that there are likely to be many ways to accomplish that goal. Finding the solution most likely to become a useful, stable, and widely supported institution is the most important goal

---

[132]IRS rules limit what can be done with those funds from tax-free bonds, and how they can be invested, but buying a CD is appropriate, so long as the interest paid isn't greater than the interest owed on the bond.

*Eight*

# Epilogue

WITH ANY LUCK, this book has provided tools and language for activists to understand their community—the business of their government(s), the state of the banking market, and the state of the local economy—and devise plans for new financial institutions to help improve the quality of life there. Like the blind men and the elephant, the economy of even a small area can be understood in many different ways, with priorities for action depending crucially on the differences. Some activists will see opportunities to relieve pressure on consumer finances, and encourage a focus on small-scale retail efforts like payday lending. Others will see deficiencies in larger credit markets and might look to establish institutions to take on wholesale functions like participation lending or market-making. Still others will look to create institutions to keep taxpayers from being victimized by financiers. Well-made plans from all those activists will likely be different from existing models, perhaps because political or financial concerns will limit their scope or perhaps just because they respond to a different set of needs.

Our nation desperately needs a new set of financial institutions, since the ones we have are not serving us well. To date, the only political response we've seen is to tighten regulations, but this is an inadequate response to banking institutions that do not acknowledge any kind of community responsibility. The problem is not that such responsibility takes too low a place on banks' priority lists; the problem is that it doesn't even appear on most of them. So long as "managing" risk remains a synonym for "find a sucker to take it" and there is no legal standard of responsibility for a bank to its customers, these problems will remain.

Imagine a world where the financial sector exists as an aid to the real economy of actual goods and services, not as a substitute for it. Where banks and investment companies exist to serve other companies, not to buy them and sell them. Where the purpose motivating bank management is to help their customers and communities, not simply to extract fees and penalties from them. We are a long way from that world at the moment. While banks themselves are not entirely responsible for the conditions of the US banking market, very few prominent bankers are doing anything at all to repair it.

As the joke goes, there is good news and bad news. The bad news is that the work of creating that world will be the work of a generation. The good news is that there are a few small signs that this work is already underway:

- The Build America Mutual bond insurance company was founded in 2012 to insure municipal bond issues. It is a mutual company, owned by its customers. In other words, several municipalities realized they could do for themselves what they have been relying on the financial industry to do for them.

- Several Occupy Wall Street activists are currently organizing the "Occupy Money" cooperative to provide banking services to poor people. Their first product is to be a pre-pay debit card meant to be an inexpensive and cooperatively-owned competitor to bank cards.

- The city of Reading, Pennsylvania, is organizing a non-profit to serve the city's banking needs, to manage the city's bank accounts and help move the city from a reliance on one huge bank to a collection of local banks willing to work closely with the city on lending initiatives.[133]

These hardly constitute a revolution, but they are encouraging signs, nonetheless. While the necessity for wholesale change in the financial landscape is obvious, the economic system of the United States has shown remarkable resilience to challenge over the past 200 years. It is not crazy to work for evolution over revolution; two centuries of experience offers little more.

Fortunately, there are ways to speed the pace of evolution. Evolution is about the survival of the most useful mutations.

---

[133]The author helped with the design of this institution. See "Service bureau" on page 152.

What we need is more mutations. We need creative people to come up with new ideas, we need activists to share those ideas and make plans, and we need organizers willing to move forward with implementing those plans. In short, what we need more than anything is a movement of people dedicated to designing and creating those new financial institutions.

History tells us about more than just the resilience of the American economic system. All of the important financial institutions that dominate our landscape began their lives as someone's idea. Elizabeth Warren's writing and relentless advocacy made the Consumer Financial Protection Bureau into a reality. Amadeo Giannini founded the Bank of Italy (which became Bank of America) in San Francisco to provide banking services for Italian immigrants who could not get service from other banks. Even Social Security had an author; it was the brainchild of Abe Epstein, the research director of the Pennsylvania Commission on Old Age Pensions in the early 1920s.

In other words, history also tells us about the remarkable creativity and depth of passion of activists who every day work to make this a better nation. We now enjoy the fruits of their hard work past. There is no reason to think this story will not continue, and that creative and motivated—and educated—activists will be the spring from which great new ideas and institutions will flow.

# Further reading

I HAVE WRITTEN this book because of the dearth of other books addressing the subject of banking in quite this way. A primer on banking is best accompanied by a history of what has happened over the past few years. There are plenty of great books about the vicissitudes of banking over the past decade, and the advent of the crisis of 2008, and I recommend you read them all.

With respect to the actual operation of banks, probably the most practically useful information out there is to be found on government web sites, and I urge everyone interested in these subjects to spend some time reading there. Both **occ.gov** and **fdic.gov** are full of useful information for current and prospective bank directors and officers. The National Credit Union Administration (NCUA) site at **ncua.gov** is equally helpful, and is aimed at novices. There is also **mycreditunion.gov**, which will help you find a set of step-by-step instructions for starting a credit union that many will find helpful. The FFIEC web site (**ffiec.gov**) is also quite useful because you can find actual reports there corresponding to things you read about and try to puzzle through how it all works that way.

Another web site worth checking out belongs to William F. Hummel, a retired aerospace engineer among whose hobbies appears to be explaining complicated finance to people. Finance can be complex, but presumably once you've mastered the dynamics of lift on a symmetrical wing section, repo transactions are no big deal. He sets out to explain banking and the money markets in plain and simple English and succeeds admirably, though careful readers will notice some quibbles I have with his accounts. Find it at **wfhummel.cnchost.com**.

Marcia Stigum's authoritative volume, "The Money Market"

whose last edition was printed in 1990 has been updated by Anthony Crescenzi, and reissued as "Stigum's Money Market" (Mcgraw-Hill, 2007). It is a comprehensive guide to the money markets that many will find quite helpful. Think of it as a tool chest for bankers.

The bible for the bond market is "The Handbook of Municipal Bonds," by Sylvan Feldstein and Frank Fabozzi (Wiley, 2008). It's a large volume and can be somewhat intimidating, but if you have a question, an authoritative answer is likely inside, and that's the most important feature for a bible, isn't it? The web site **publicbonds.org** has a lot of useful information, too, and Emma, the MSRB web site at **emma.msrb.org** is a great companion to these.

Some other random volumes I have found useful and interesting include these:

- "A Call for Judgment: Sensible Finance for a Dynamic Economy" by Amar Bhidé (Oxford, 2010). An interesting analysis with prescriptions you don't often see.

- "Analyzing Banking Risk: A Framework for Assessing Corporate Governance and Financial Risk Management" by Hennie van Greuning and Sonja Brajovic Bratanovic (World Bank, 2000). A more comprehensive look at the varieties of bank risk, with useful thoughts about how to tell if a bank is dealing with risk or ignoring it.

- "Ten Lessons Bankers Never Learn: How Banks Operate and Why Bankers Screw Up" by Courtney Dufries (iUniverse, 2011). Dufries, a longtime bank regulator and regulatory consultant, writes some war stories, some history, and some explanation. A good read, but not really a primer.

# Acknowledgments

I HAVE TO ACKNOWLEDGE a debt to two fine men who are no longer around to see the fruits of their assistance. Miguel Luna was a City Council member in Providence, Rhode Island, and one of the merriest troublemakers I've had the pleasure of working with. Miguel was merciless in badgering me into helping him with a banking proposal, and it was simply easier to comply than resist. His insistence, and things that happened along that way, explain a great deal of what you hold in your hands now. Tom Hogg, the longtime CFO of Rhode Island Housing, a creative and gentle man, offered so much more than just several excellent ideas in our few encounters. In very different ways, both were able to direct my gaze beyond the horizon, to consider what might be possible instead of just what is usually done. I am forever grateful to them both.

Much of the research for this book was done in the course of my work designing banking proposals for various municipalities and counties. Because my conversations with bankers and bank regulators were initiated for different purposes, it would not be appropriate to name them here. And some regulators who I did ask for help with this book asked me not to name them, lest I give the impression that their agency has endorsed it.[134] It would, however, be appropriate to thank them for the time they spent helping me understand the constraints under which any bank must operate. My conversations with the regulators—at several different agencies—were always very revealing, and I urge any-

---

[134] And here's where the fractured and crazy nature of US bank regulation becomes an advantage, because I can say that the regulators who helped me came from multiple federal and multiple state agencies and you'll still have no idea which ones I mean.

one considering any kind of banking proposal to call up the relevant regulators early and often.

I owe a special debt to Stephen Tall, now of Acadia Trust, for sharing with me so much of his hard work and plenty of his time, too. I am lucky to have such a friend. And Mark Binder, my friend and editor, has been an invaluable partner in making this book happen. Marc Armstrong, of the Public Banking Institute, invited me to give a workshop on banking fundamentals, and much of this book grew out of that effort. Garry Bliss, Marco Vangelisti, Carla Rautenberg, and my favorite proofreader all helped me find typos and omissions and generally squeeze out the stupid. They are all due my thanks, as well as the obligatory relief from responsibility: Any errors you find within the book are all mine.

# Glossary

THIS BOOK IS DESIGNED to *be* a glossary. However, it is also an introduction and it is sometimes inconvenient to put a definition right at the first appearance of a term. I recommend the index, which will usually take you to a definition in context. But this glossary will help, too. The parenthesized page numbers point to where the term is defined in the text.

## #

**100% reserve banking**   A way to disguise banking for those who are uncomfortable with the risks involved in maturity transformation. (40)

## A

**accounting capital**   Whatever is owned by a bank. That is, whatever is possessed by a bank, and not owed to some other party. (18)

**accounting equation**   The accounting equation is what balances a balance sheet. All the assets added up has to equal all the liabilities plus all the capital. Another way to look at it is just to say that assets—what a bank/company/person *has*—is always and by definition equal to what they *own* plus what they *owe* to others. This is always and forever true. Accountants use the equation to make sure they've done their work right, not to see whether the equation is actually satisfied. (15)

**accredited investors**   The SEC's term of art to refer to investors who are rich enough, and therefore supposedly sophisticated enough, that they don't need consumer protection. These are the people and institutions allowed to invest in otherwise un-regulated venture capital, private equity, and hedge funds. This includes not just rich people, but pension funds, government money managers, foundations, and so on. (74)

**ACH**   Automated Clearing House, an electronic payment system equivalent to a check. ACH transactions are "netted" and presented for payment after some time, just like a check clearing process. (78)

**Alt-A**   A mortgage industry classification for loans to buyers who might not qualify for a "prime" loan, but whose credit is better than necessary for a "sub-prime" loan. Also known as "liar loans" for the lack of documentation required to apply for one. (5)

**arbitrage**   Taking advantage of a difference in price between two markets. For example, if US dollars are selling for 0.7 GBP in London and 0.65 GBP in Amsterdam, you can make money through arbitrage, by buying dollars in Amsterdam and selling them in London. Markets aren't necessarily geographic. The mortgage lending market is different from the market for savings accounts. The interest rate prevailing in the mortgage lending market is usually different than the interest rate prevailing in the market for savings accounts. Therefore, a bank can "buy" deposits and "sell" loans to make money. This kind of interest-rate arbitrage is what plain-vanilla banks do. (42)

**ARC**   The Actuarially Required Contribution for a pension fund is whatever the actuaries say is the right amount to contribute to a fund to meet its obligations into the future. (126)

**ask price**   A broker's "ask price" is the price at which he or she will sell you some security. The "bid price" is the price at which he or she will buy it. (131)

**assessment**   The FDIC uses this word for the insurance premiums they charge banks. Bank assessments pay for deposit insurance, not taxes. (93)

**asset statement**   Another name, typically used by governments, for a balance sheet. (123)

**assets**   A company's assets are the things it *has*. This includes both things it owns and things it owes to other people or companies. (Also known as the capital and liabilities.) For

a bank, the assets are its loans, and whatever investments it
has made, along with its offices, furniture, carpets in the CEO
suite, limousines, and private jets. It also will include intangible stuff like trademarks and other intellectual property, and
even less tangible stuff like reputation and good will. (16)

**AUM**    A bank or investment company might report "Assets Under Management:" the assets it owns as well as the assets it
might be managing for others. A money market fund, for
example, where investors buy shares, will be mainly com-
posed of assets owned by those investors, but managed by
the fund. (98)

# B

**balance sheet**    A statement of a bank's assets on one side of the
ledger (tradition puts it on the left and who are we to question tradition?) and the capital and liabilities on the other
side. Because the accounting equation says the two sides
have to be equal, the sheet is said to "balance." Remember
that the accounting equation is a definition, so if you have a
balance sheet where the two sides are not equal, you're doing
it wrong. (15)

**bank equity capital**    A synonym for accounting capital: the stuff
owned by the bank and not owed to anyone else. (18)

**Bank of North Dakota**    A state-owned bank, the only publicly-
owned bank in the United States. Founded by radical pop-
ulists in 1919, it rapidly became an indispensable part of the
state's economy, and was almost immediately embraced by
the very same conservatives who won office by vowing to
shut it down. (32)

**bank run**    A period of great excitement at a bank, where no one
knows whether the bank has enough cash in the till to give
to the crowd of frenzied customers demanding their money
back. No bank keeps all its money in its safe, so a bank run
can devastate even a well-managed bank. (46)

**banker's bank**    A bank designed to offer services to other banks.
Usually these are the kinds of services that little banks can't
really afford to do for themselves, but there are other reasons
why a bank might turn to a third party for some services. (71)

**Basel Accords**   A series of international banking agreements meant to increase the stability of the global financial system. You'll see them as Basel I, Basel II, and Basel III (dating from 1988, 2004, and 2011, respectively). You can use this book to decode discussions about the adequacy of the various Basel regulations, but this book can't possibly hold a discussion of them all. Suffice to say that the intent of the Basel Accords is noble, but they have too often undercut by bank lobbying, and then used as a way to beat back further regulation by national authorities. It is therefore not at all clear whether they are a net positive to the global system. (25)

**basis points**   A hundredth of a percentage point. The difference between 3.74% and 3.79% is five basis points. (49)

**bid price**   A broker's "bid price" is the price at which he or she will buy some security you wish to sell. The "ask price" is the price at which he or she will sell it. (131)

**BIS**   The Bank for International Settlements is sort of the world's central bank for central banks. (81)

**bitcoin**   As of 2013, a relatively new, mysterious, and imaginative form of electronic currency that, unlike other forms of electronic payments, can be used with 100% anonymity. This has made it popular among those who crave anonymity, for good and ill. (82)

**BND**   See Bank of North Dakota. (32)

**bond insurance**   A city or county (or company) that would like to issue a bond can purchase bond insurance in order to reduce the risk of default on the bond and thereby get a better (lower) interest rate. This only works if the insurance company has a better bond rating than the bond issuer. (135)

**brokered deposits**   A securities broker can offer shares in some large CD at a bank, just the way they might offer a share of a company or of a bond. Some banks rely heavily on this kind of deposit (and this kind of deposit is available to investment banks). Despite the fixed term, brokered deposits can be fairly volatile, and so FDIC rules prevent banks that are not "well-capitalized" from using them. Growth in reliance on brokered deposits is seldom a good sign for a bank. (61)

**budget reserve**   A budget reserve consists of a government's unbudgeted funds. These may or may not ever exist as actual money, depending on how accurately the budget predicts the future. Contrast this with a cash reserve. (122)

**buy-back agreement**  A collateralized loan masked as two purchase agreements. For example I might buy a car from you for $1000 at the same time I promise to sell it back to you tomorrow for $1001. You get $1000 for a day and I make a dollar in profit. This is more or less the same thing as a repo transaction, but usually appears in a different context, such as Islamic banking. (39)

# C

**CAFR**  A Comprehensive Annual Financial Report contains an accounting of the finances of a government, and includes some of the various almost-independent entities that make up that government: pension funds, water authorities, transportation agencies, and so on. (123)

**call report**  Officially a "Consolidated Report on Condition and Income," the call report is a quarterly summary of a bank's condition. The name comes from an earlier practice of having the bank regulators "call" for a report on a date chosen by surprise, a practice that lasted until the 1960s. Find call reports for any bank condensed into the "Uniform Bank Performance Reports" at ffiec.gov. (91)

**capital**  In an accounting sense, it's what a bank owns itself and doesn't owe to anyone else. In a financial sense, it's the amount of money a bank can lose before being forced to stiff its creditors. (Depositors among them.) These are obviously related concepts, but they are not the same thing, which causes endless confusion and is partly why this book exists. (17)

**capital appreciation bond**  Like a zero-coupon bond, but the face value is the purchase price, not the payout amount, so the accounting is different for the issuer. (140)

**CAR**  The "Capital Adequacy Ratio" is the ratio of a bank's capital to its invested assets. Ratios larger than about 10% are considered healthy by US bank regulators, though earlier times would have defined "healthy" more rigorously. (24)

**cash reserve**  A pool of cash (or cash equivalent) intended to make whatever payments have to be made over some period under some worst-case scenario. For a government, this extra can also be called a rainy day fund. Do not confuse with a budget reserve. (122)

**CD**  A certificate of deposit, a kind of time deposit, usually with a penalty for early withdrawal if early withdrawal is possible at all. (19)

**CDARS**  A system of cooperating banks who share each others' large deposits so that deposits stay below the FDIC insurance limit of $250,000. (127)

**CDFI**  A Community Development Financial Institution focuses on community economic development. Ranging from tiny loan funds run by a community development corporation (CDC) to credit unions and banks, the CDFI program is a way for the Treasury Department to give small community-oriented programs a small advantage in accessing services used by banks. (151)

**CDO**  A Collateralized Debt Obligation is any security whose income derives from the income of debts held "within" the security. An MBS is a CDO. (56)

**CDS**  See "credit default swap." (65)

**CFPB**  The Consumer Financial Protection Bureau was created via the Dodd-Frank legislation, it is housed at the Fed, and is charged with regulating the consumer-facing side of banking: consumer accounts, credit and debit cards, and so on. The brainchild of Elizabeth Warren, its director is Richard Corddray because Republicans in the Senate insisted she would not be confirmed as its director. She is now Senator from Massachusetts, instead. (91)

**CFTC**  The Commodity Futures Trading Commission is charged with regulating the nation's commodities markets. Derivatives like futures options were invented to deal with commodities trading, so the commodities markets attracts traders who want to use those tools to create new financial products. Consequently the CFTC has some authority over derivatives, though not much. Exactly how much influence they have is a current subject of debate. (90)

**CHIPS** Clearing House Interbank Payment System is a private clearing house that also operates an international wire transfer system. There are only about 50 members, but these are some of the biggest banks in the world. Most of them are based outside the US, and so CHIPS makes a great route for international payments. (77)

**clearing** The process by which a check or electronic debit finds its way back to its mother bank, to be debited to the account of the customer who wrote it. (76)

**clearing house** A clearing house is a organization that takes a pile of checks and sorts and delivers them to the banks on which they were written. A clearing house can also refer to a "netting engine" which takes a large number of drafts or funds transfers and reduces them to a smaller number of interbank transfers. Most clearing houses provide both functions. (76)

**closed-end investment company** An investment company no longer open to new investors. Also sometimes called simply "closed." Compare to open-end. (72)

**commercial bank** A commercial bank once meant a bank focused on lending to businesses. But these days, thrifts make business loans and commercial banks make home loans, so the distinction between a commercial bank and a savings bank is difficult to detect. (107)

**commercial paper** Short term corporate (sometimes government) bonds with a maturity of less than 270 days. Only typically used by corporations or governments with the best bond ratings. (55)

**community bank** Typically a smaller bank, a community bank has a commitment to the community it supports. Contrast this to a large money center bank. (53)

**concentration risk** Too many eggs in too few baskets. (47)

**cost of funds** Banker shorthand for the implied interest rate to cover the whole borrowing cost of some class of funds. For deposits, for example, the cost of funds would include the administrative costs of running the bank branches and account management functions. If the cost of running 5 bank branches is a million dollars a year, and the branches yield

$50 million in deposits, one might say that the cost of funds is 2%. Because it is expressed as an interest rate, it allows for easy comparison to whatever interest rate those funds might earn. (17)

**coupon bond**   A typical bond pays interest twice a year over the bond term, then repays the principal at the end. This is sometimes known as a coupon bond because once upon a time, the bond came with coupons attached that the bondholder would clip off and send in for redemption. A "coupon-clipper" was therefore, someone living off bond proceeds, typically the dissipated scion of some industrial pioneer, living out his days in a cafe in the Greek isles. (129)

**coupon rate**   The stated interest rate for some bond. (129)

**CRA**   The Community Reinvestment Act was an act of Congress passed in the 1970s that set out geographic standards for lending. Under CRA requirements, a bank has a responsibility to serve all of the neighborhoods of its lending area. (91)

**CRAR**   The Capital Risk-weighted Asset Ratio is like a CAR, but uses risk-weighted assets (see "RWA") instead of assets. It is, unfortunately, a hybrid measure that mushes two very different concepts—the riskiness of a bank's capital structure, and the riskiness of its assets—into a single number, for better and worse. (28)

**credit card association**   The governing body for a credit card brand. Visa, MasterCard, and Discover are credit card associations. (78)

**credit default swap**   A swap of credit default risk. This is basically an insurance policy against the default of some credit risk. The important points about a CDS are that: first, you don't have to own the asset that might suffer the default you're insuring against, and second, the bank that offers to insure your risk is subject to nothing in the way of insurance regulation. The history of the insurance industry tells us that is a very bad idea, but somehow that wasn't thought to be relevant to banking when CDS regulation was proposed in the 1990s. (65)

**credit rating agency**   A company that issues credit ratings for bonds and other credit risks. Typically the ratings agencies are paid by the bond issuers, but are supposed to trusted by the bond buyers. The identity of who it was, exactly, who thought that was a good idea has been lost in the mists of time. (134)

**credit risk** The most basic kind of banking risk: give someone a loan and they might not pay it back. (24)

**credit union** A depositor-owned financial institution that can do small consumer loans: mortgages, car loans, credit cards, and so on. These are typically organized around some common interest. A credit union might be open to employees of some company or members of some union or association. Credit unions are fairly limited in the forms of business they can pursue. Mutual banks are a similar idea. (145)

**current yield** The annual amount returned by a bond, divided by the bond price. A bond with a face value of $1000 and coupon rate of 5%, if it was bought for $800, would produce a current yield of around 6.25%. (129)

**CUSIP number** The CUSIP number is a serial number that uniquely identifies every security sold in the US. Stands for Committee on Uniform Security Identification Procedures, an organization founded inthe 1960s. (130)

# D

**de novo bank** A startup bank, rendered in Latin for some reason, presumably to scare off intruders. (52)

**debenture** The agreement governing a bond. This spells out who owes what to whom and under what conditions and how the money is to be spent and the whole thing. Usually requires a bevy of attorneys to construct. (131)

**debit card** A card that offers a way to pay directly out of a demand deposit account. Sometimes called a plastic check. (79)

**demand deposit** A deposit account whose funds are available to the depositor on demand. A checking account is a demand deposit, as are simple savings accounts. Contrast this with a "time deposit" like a CD. (19)

**discount rate** There are two meanings of this word. "The" discount rate is the interest rate charged by the Fed for loans from the discount window. It can also mean the rate of interest used in a present value calculation, such as are often made when making pension fund predictions. (64)

**discount window**   A source of short-term loans made directly by the Fed to any of its member banks. Usually a bank can get a better deal borrowing from other banks in the Fed funds market, so the discount window is usually only used by banks under some cloud of suspicion. (63)

**draft**   An order from a depositor that a bank pay a certain amount from the depositor's account. A check is the most common form of draft. (76)

**DTCC**   The Depository Trust and Clearing Corporation is a trust that holds most of the securities bought and sold in the US. By holding all the securities in one place, they can be traded just by moving electronic credits from one account to another instead of trading pieces of paper. (80)

# E

**enterprise fund**   A term for a part of a government supported by fees for services rendered, as opposed to being supported by taxes. A sewer fund, supported by sewer fees, would count as an enterprise fund. (119)

**equity**   The same thing as accounting capital. (17)

# F

**Fannie Mae**   The Federal National Mortgage Association is the largest of the "Government Sponsored Enterprises" (GSEs). Designed to promote homeownership by relieving banks of some of their long-term credit risk, Fannie Mae is, as of 2014, the largest purchaser of bank mortgages on the secondary market. Fannie started life as a government operation during the Great Depression. It was privatized in 1968, and then taken over by the government during the 2008 financial crisis. (56)

**FASB**   The Financial Accounting Standards Board is a committee of accountants that sets the rules by which private corporations are audited and how they report their finances. FASB creates the GAAP for private corporations. (89)

**FDIC**   The Federal Deposit Insurance Corporation was created during the Great Depression to insure bank deposits and prevent bank runs. The FDIC assesses a premium from its member banks (called an assessment), and provides the insurance from its trust fund. The independent FDIC is presumably backed by the US Government, but hasn't had to tap that line of credit yet, despite some close shaves. (92)

**Fed**   The Federal Reserve is the central bank for the USA. It holds the reserve funds of all its member banks, sets monetary policy for the nation, regulates bank holding companies and state-chartered banks, and clears all the checks. Among other things. (68)

**Fed funds**   Bank reserve funds kept at the Federal Reserve, the US central bank, are called Fed funds. Banks loan these funds to each other all the time, in the "Fed funds market." The interest rate for these loans is set by the Fed, and is one of the few (but potent) controls the bank has over the nation's economy. (68)

**Fedwire**   The Federal Reserve's wire transfer system, used to move money from one bank to another. (77)

**FFIEC**   The Federal Financial Institutions Examination Council is an association of the Federal bank regulating agencies. It tries to promote a uniform approach to bank regulation among the federal agencies involved. Its web site is the best source for bank financial data, not least because you don't have to remember which agency is the regulator for the bank you're looking for: ffiec.gov. (91)

**FHA**   The Federal Housing Administration is one of the big mortgage insurers in the US. As such, they have an outsized effect on the mortgage market, since the standards they set for insurability determine whether loans can be resold on the secondary market to Fannie Mae or Freddie Mac. (58)

**FHLB**   The Federal Home Loan Bank is a giant mutual banker's bank, with twelve branches, somewhat like the Fed, but specifically designed to provide liquidity to banks who make home mortgage loans. (69)

**FHLMC**   See "Freddie Mac." (56)

**financial capital**   The amount of money a bank can lose before being forced to stiff its creditors. Often just called "capital." This is a different concept than equity capital (which is also often just called "capital"), though it's obviously related. The "tiers" of capital are an attempt to create real definitions for financial capital. See "Tier 1 capital." (24)

**FINRA**   The Financial Industry Regulatory Authority is a private regulatory agency, owned and operated by the securities firms it regulates. (89)

**FNMA**   See "Fannie Mae." (56)

**fractional reserve banking**   This is just another name for banking as we know it, where a bank loans (or invests) the bulk of the deposits it receives, and keeps a fraction of it on reserve to satisfy customer demands for cash. (38)

**Freddie Mac**   Who knows why the Federal Home Loan Mortgage Company came to be called Freddie Mac, but it did. Along with the larger Fannie Mae, it is one of the GSE's designed to increase the availability of 30-year fixed-rate mortgages. Unlike Fannie, Freddie Mac was started as a private enterprise, and remained that way until it was taken over by the government during the financial crisis of 2008. (56)

**full reserve banking**   See "100% reserve banking." (40)

**fund balance**   The difference between assets and liabilities for a government or non-profit, where tradition demands we don't call it "capital." (123)

**funding ratio**   In pension accounting, the ratio of the assets to the net present value of the future liabilities, calculated out to some horizon, usually 30 years. Generally speaking this is a more meaningful number than the UAAL (unfunded liability), but the UAAL is often used to induce a sense of panic in the audience. (125)

# G

**GAAP**   The Generally Accepted Accounting Principles are a set of rules to use in reporting the finances of a corporation or government. They are set by FASB and GASB, respectively. Accountants argue vociferously amongst themselves about the proper rules, but they get very touchy when outsiders question those rules. (89)

**GASB** The Governmental Accounting Standards Board is FASB for government. GASB sets the GAAP for reporting government finances. (89)

**general fund** In government accounting, the general fund is the main repository of taxes and source of expense payments. The best definition defines it by what it is not: restricted funds. The legislative body in charge of that government has wide latitude for spending general funds. (121)

**general obligation bond** A bond backed by the full credit of some government. Compare to a revenue bond. (132)

**Ginnie Mae** The Government National Mortgage Association was started in 1968, when Fannie Mae was privatized. Ginnie Mae was created to undertake Fannie's activities that would have been awkward to assign to a private entity, such as guaranteeing bonds backed by government-subsidized mortgages. (56)

**GNMA** Ginnie Mae (56)

**GSE** The Government-Sponsored Enterprises are Fannie Mae and Freddie Mac, and Ginnie Mae. Fannie and Freddie were private organizations started by the government to create a secondary market for mortgages, and were widely perceived as having the implicit backing of the government, which allowed them to borrow at very low cost. They almost failed during the 2008 financial crisis and were taken over by the federal government which operates them now. (56)

# H

**hedge fund** Originally an investment company that followed a specific hedging strategy designed to give modest but consistent gains to its investors. Has come to be less specific and now essentially just refers to an unregulated investment company open to accredited investors and following a wide variety of investment strategies. (74)

**heteroskedasticity** A collection of variables where some portion of the population measured has a different variability than others. For example, a population of wild horses could include one family that is all tan and another where some are black and some are tan. A population where the variability is consistent among all the sub-populations is homoskedastic. So now you can show off your command of statistics jargon. (95)

**humility**  A quality you would expect to see more of from economists and bankers who failed to foresee the disasters of 2007–2008. See SOSD. (87)

# I

**IFRS**  International Financial Reporting Standards are the accounting standards used for banks in Europe. This is the international version of GAAP, for banks and other financial institutions. (101)

**imputed interest**  A non-interest cost, divided by some funds, can be expressed as an interest rate, and this is "imputed" interest. See "cost of funds." (17)

**income statement**  An integral part of a set of financial reports, showing the amounts and sources of its income. Also called the P&L statement. (22)

**information asymmetry**  Best illustrated by offering to sell you a car from New Jersey after hurricane Sandy. Lots of cars on used car lots were flooded by salt water, but a buyer has no idea which ones were flooded (and will therefore be a disaster to buy) and which ones stayed dry. This is information asymmetry, when one side of a transaction (or potential transaction) knows a lot more than the other about the goods on sale. Information aysmmetry can affect a whole market. Even if only a small fraction of cars were inundated with salt, the price of all of them went down because no one can be sure some particular car wasn't flooded. (103)

**interchange fee**  See "swipe fee." (45)

**interest rate risk**  A variety of market risk. In the 1970s, many banks found themselves having to pay interest rates of 10–12% on their deposits while they had a base of mortgage loans paying around 6–7% in income. These banks were experiencing the downside of interest rate risk. The banks that sold Philadelphia those interest rate swaps experienced the upside. (46)

**interest rate swap**  An agreement to exchange debt payments. A bank might approach a city and offer to swap payments on some of their fixed-rate debt for the city's floating rate debt. The bank would pay the city a fee, subtract its expenses, and then make the city's debt payments, while the city paid the bank's. The bank is relieved of some of its interest rate risk, while the city gets a fee. Of course, it doesn't always work out well, as we've seen in Philadelphia. (65)

**investment bank**   A bank with neither depositors nor the regulation that goes along with them. Investment banks were originally small associations of wealthy individuals who pooled that wealth to pursue a wide variety of business opportunities, which included borrowing and lending, but also investing in new businesses. In the 1970s, some of the nation's investment banks dramatically increased their funding by becoming public corporations and selling stock. (72)

**investment company**   A company formed to accumulate funds from many investors and invest them collectively. (72)

**Islamic banking**   Banks arranged around the Koran's prohibition of usury. (39)

# L

**laddered investment**   Arranging a set of investments so that at any one time there isn't long to wait until one of them matures. For example, imagine 12 one-year CDs staggered so that one of them matures each month. (151)

**letter of credit**   A bank's endorsement of one of its customers (available for a fee). For a bond transaction, this allows an issuer to use the bank's credit rating for its bonds. Letters of credit expire, however, and often have a term of only a few years, far shorter than many bonds. (43)

**leverage**   In a financial sense, leverage is using a small amount of money to reap the benefit of investing a larger amount. A bank leverages its capital with customer deposits. (36)

**leverage ratio**   A measure of how little money is actually invested in a deal. The lower the leverage ratio, the higher the risk. For a bank, the leverage ratio is the ratio of capital to assets. (36)

**liability**   In an accounting sense, a liability is simply something

you owe. In banking, banks owe a liability to their depositors, and to anyone else from whom they borrow. This does
sometimes seem a little odd, since when someone deposits
$100 into a bank, the bank winds up with a $100 liability. But
they also wind up with a $100 asset, so the balance is main-
tained. (17)

**liar loans**   See "Alt-A loans", also "NINJA loans." (104)

**LIBOR**   The London InterBank Offered Rate is a benchmark interest rate. Interest rates around the world are referenced to
the LIBOR rate. More important, lots of interest rate swap
deals reference the rate. For several years, a number of
the world's largest banks were manipulating the rate, in order to make deals that referenced the rate more favorable to
them. (142)

**liquidity risk**   The chance that a bank won't have enough cash
on hand to meet the demand from its creditors. Liquidity risk
sometimes manifests itself as a bank run, but any action by
creditors to demand cash that a bank doesn't possess would
be a liquidity event. (46)

**loan loss allowance**   On a bank's balance sheet, the value of a
bank's loan assets should always be reduced from its face
value by the amount of loans expected to default. For example, a bank owed $100 million by its borrowers would show
$95 million in loan value if it expects 5% of its loans to default.
The loan loss allowance is typically shown as a negative asset.
You'll also see this as a "loan loss reserve." (33)

**LOC**   See "letter of credit." (43)

**lockbox service**   A lockbox is service banks offer to businesses
and governments that get a lot of payments by mail. It is little
more than an address to which people can send checks, and
a staff there to open envelopes and deposit the checks found
within them. A county government might use a lockbox to
receive property tax payments or sewer bills. Many lockbox
services also print and send out the bills. (44)

# M

**market maker**   An investor or investment bank that commits to
be always willing to buy some security. They need not buy it

at any particular price, though. A bank or investment company will commit to being a market maker in order to sell some security, so that potential customers know they can get rid of it down the line if they need to. It's essentially a marketing enticement, not much different from a store that promises to allow you to return the sweater you bought there. (131)

**market risk** The risk that market forces will change the value of some asset a bank holds. A climate of declining real estate prices exposes banks who hold mortgages to market risk. Interest rate risk is a variety of market risk. (46)

**maturity transformation** A bank takes in short-term deposits and makes long-term loans, transforming the money's function. (40)

**MBS** A mortgage-backed security is a bond with income derived from the mortgage payments of homeowners whose mortgages are packaged within the bond. (56)

**money center bank** A large, impersonal, international bank. The biggest banks provide a lot of liquidity to smaller banks through the Fed funds and repo markets, but their size, the impossibility of guarantee, and the reckless nature with which they have conducted themselves over recent decades counterbalance their positive contributions. (53)

**money market fund** An investment fund, usually open-ended, that invests in short-term money market securities. A money market fund usually tries to keep its share price at $1, to facilitate customers exiting and entering the fund. (73)

**moral obligation bond** A bond written on a subsidiary of some government is often said to impose a moral obligation on the government, even if the bond debenture specifically says otherwise. An example might be a bond issued by a county economic development authority to build a shopping mall, with the bond debt to be repaid by the increased property taxes from the nearby commercial property (this is called "Tax Increment Financing"). If the mall never gets built because it would impinge on valuable painted turtle habitat, the bonds can't be repaid. Bankers will then insist the county has a "moral obligation" to repay the bonds, and the bond rating agencies will threaten to downgrade the county's bond rating to force the county to honor the bonds. (133)

**morality**  In banking, morality appears to be defined this way: customers are bad people if they don't pay back their loans, and bankers are bad people if they don't take every available advantage to make money. From their customers, of course. How else to explain the lionization of bank presidents whose banks have been repeatedly fined for breaking laws and the condemnation of people whose homes have been foreclosed upon? (39)

**MSRB**  The Municipal Securities Rulemaking Board is an association of municipal bond brokers and dealers. Like most self-regulators, its record is a mixed bag, but its web site, emma.msrb.org is fabulous, both a great source of data about specific bonds, and also a good resource for people learning about bonds. (90)

**multiplier**  For people interested in the money creation aspect of banking, the theoretical maximum amount of money created by a banking system is the inverse of the reserve requirement. So if the reserve requirement is 10%, the multiplier is a factor of 10. A million dollars deposited into a banking system under these conditions would produce a ten million dollar increase in the money supply. The theoretical maximum is almost never achieved, due to leakage, differing bank business strategies, uneven demand for loans, maturity mismatches, and much more. (84)

**municipal bond**  A government bond from any US government besides *the* US government: cities, towns, counties, states, economic development authorities, water systems, zoos, port authorities, power systems, and all the rest. (130)

**municipal bond bank**  Many cities and towns are either too small or too poor to have access to the bond market. A bond bank is a way for their governments to pool their resources and have access to that enormous source of funds. The bond bank is the debtor of record in the bond transaction (and so receives the bond rating). It issues bonds, and then lends the resulting funds to the member cities, towns, counties, whatever. (135)

**mutual bank**  An unjustly neglected form of bank, where the depositors own the bank. Mutual banks are out of fashion now because no one gets rich with a mutual bank, but they are (or could be) very useful institutions, designed at a time when banking was a means to an end, not the end itself. With a mutual bank, certain depositors "pledge" deposits for a longish term, and those count as the capital of the bank. Those accounts don't earn interest, but owners of the pledged deposits can get a dividend. Mutual banks are not as limited as credit unions in the forms of business they can undertake. They can do most of what any other banks does. (145)

**mutual fund**   An investment company generally with a fairly low threshold for investors. There are mutual funds that invest in all kinds of things, from financial instruments to commodities and real estate. Most funds are open-ended, but some are closed, either by design or circumstance. (73)

# N

**netting**   There are two meanings for netting. The first is just what a clearing house does, condense a large number of small transactions among a group of banks into a small number of large transactions. It can also mean a sneaky way for a bank to shrink its balance sheet and hide leverage. The idea is that, for certain derivative investments, if a bank owes a debt to some other bank but that second bank owes money to the first bank, you need only account for the net value of the two debts. In an accounting sense, this makes some sense. It can also make two precarious banks look like two solid banks, so in a legal, realistic, and practical sense, not so much. (101)

**NINJA**   No Income, No Job or Assets. See "liar loans." (104)

**non-bank banks**   See "shadow bank." (101)

**note**   A short term bond, usually with a maturity less than five years. For the US Treasury, notes of term less than a year are typically called "bills" or "T-bills." (55)

**NRSRO**   A Nationally Recognized Statistical Rating Organization is one of the big three ratings agencies: Standard & Poor's, Moody's, and Fitch. (134)

**NSS**   The National Settlement Service is a Fed-operated service that takes a collection of payment instructions, generally output from some clearing house, and executes them. A clearing house might take a thousand checks among three banks and net them into three transactions. They then forward a description of those three transactions to NSS, who executes them. (76)

# O

**OCC**   The Office of the Comptroller of the Currency is part of the Treasury Department, and regulates national banks, among other things. (88)

**off-balance sheet**   An asset or liability that need not be recorded on a bank's balance sheet. An agreement to lend money tomorrow would be an off-balance sheet asset, since the balance sheet has no way to account for a transaction that hasn't happened yet, but exists in a legal sense. Assets and liabilities that don't appear on the accounts sound shady, and often is, but is not necessarily so. Unfortunately, telling the difference between the shady and legitimate uses is tricky, and creates loopholes large enough to drive freight trains through. See "SIV." (98)

**OPEB**   Short for Other Post-Employment Benefits, usually meaning health care for retirees. Two GASB circulars of the early 2000s dramatically changed how governments are supposed to account for these expenses. (125)

**open market operations**   The way the Fed (or any other central bank) affects interest rates and the money supply in the economy. The Fed buys and sells government securities in its own portfolio to affect the supply of money and therefore the interest rate. To see how it works, imagine what happens to the supply of money in the world when the Fed sells a billion dollars of securities. The Fed gives the bonds to the purchasers, takes their money, and withdraws it from the economy. When the Fed buys bonds, it injects more money into the economy. (68)

**open repo**   A repo transaction that can be rolled over indefinitely. At least the borrowing bank hopes so. (64)

**open-end investment company**   An investment company open to new customers with enough money to invest in it. Compare to closed-end. (72)

**operational risk**   This is the risk that something may go wrong that has nothing to do with lending or any of the bank's core business. This could be embezzlement, being fined by the SEC, floods, enraged depositors vandalizing bank branches, lightning strikes and so on. (47)

**OTC**  This stands for Over The Counter and is used for any kind of security or commodity that is *not* traded on an exchange. OTC transactions are not really monitored by anyone and are really just legal agreements between two parties. The bond market is an OTC kind of market, as are most derivatives. (Commodities futures are traded on the commodities exchanges.) (72)

**OTS**  The Office of Thrift Supervision is defunct. It existed to regulate "thrifts" consumer-oriented savings banks that made home mortgages and did other consumerish lending. OTS was one of the prime offenders in the agonizingly weak financial regulation that contributed to the 2008 financial crisis, and it was closed by the Dodd-Frank legislation. (88)

**over the counter**  See "OTC." (72)

# P

**P&L statement**  A "profit and loss" statement. See "income statement." (22)

**PACE loan**  A Property Assessed Clean Energy loan is a small loan for energy efficiency measures (usually insulation or efficiency improvements to HVAC equipment, but also for small-scale solar or wind power). The idea behind a PACE loan is that it is repaid through a property assessment, billed with the property tax bill. As of 2013, the FHA has turned up its nose at mortgages on properties with PACE liens on them, so the idea is having trouble getting off the ground. (58)

**payday lender**  A business that makes small short-term loans. A typical payday lender might offer a two-week loan of $100 for $10, which might sound reasonable until you do the math and realize it's an interest rate of 260%. Payday lenders are common in poor neighborhoods (of states without effective usury laws), often as part of a check-cashing business. (155)

**payment system**  A way to get money from one party to another. Authoritative estimates say there are approximately a zillion different kinds, ranging from a simple exchange of cash, to credit cards, debit cards, ACH, checks, wire transfers, and on and on. (75)

**pension fund**   A big pile of money, the accumulated wealth of a pension system, with fewer restrictions on investments than is usual in government. GASB changes to accounting rules in the 1990s are forcing governments across the country to make these funds much bigger than necessary to pay pensions, increasing the cost of government, but it makes the accountants, bankers, and investment advisors happy, and isn't that what really counts? (125)

**pledged deposits**   See "mutual bank." (145)

**PMI**   Private mortgage insurance. (58)

**POS**   Stands for "Point Of Sale." Usually implies a credit card terminal (where you slide your card) or a cash register. (80)

**positive pay**   A checking account service where the account owner forwards to the bank a list of all the checks written, and the bank agrees to honor only those checks. (76)

**present value**   The present value of some sum of money in the future is the amount of money you would have to have today, invested in some reasonable way, to get that money in the future. The yield of the reasonable investment is called the "discount rate." The present value of $1000 a year with a discount rate of 5% is $952 because $952 invested for a year at that interest rate will yield $1000 at the end of the year. (125)

**price banking**   What happens after the demise of "relationship banking," where customers just go to whatever bank or financial institution has the best price for its services. The demise has already happened in many places. (11)

**primary credit**   One of the categories of credit available at the Federal Reserve's "discount window." These are short-term loans, for terms ranging from overnight to a month or so. Primary credit is loaned at the "discount rate." (64)

**private equity fund**   An investment company whose purpose is to make investments in corporations, take control of them, and manage them for "shareholder value." In practice, this generally means exploiting distortions of the tax laws that favor debt payments over dividends and management that elevates short-term concerns over the long-term health of the company or its employees. (74)

**private-label bank**   A bank willing to provide banking services for a non-bank that wants to pretend it is a bank. (71)

# R

**rainy day fund**   See "cash reserve."   Don't see "budget reserve." (122)

**RAN**   A Revenue Anticipation Note. Same as a "TAN." (55)

**refunding bond**   In the bond world, refinancing a bond is called "refunding" the bond. A municipality might refund a bond to tak advantage of lower interest rates, or to retire some debt. (133)

**regulatory risk**   When regulations change, a bank's business changes, too. If capital requirements change, there will be some cost to accommodating the new regulation, and some banks may not be able to. (47)

**relationship banking**   Banking where the bankers actually know their customers and use that knowledge in assessing the risks of their lending. Contrast with "price banking" and using mathematical models to tell you who is a good credit risk. (11)

**repo transaction**   A loan masquerading as two purchases. I "sell" you a bunch of securities for money, plus an agreement to buy them back from you tomorrow. The securities act as collateral for the loan, in case I change my mind or become insolvent before I buy them back. (64)

**repurchase agreement**   See "repo transaction." (64)

**reserve requirements**   There are two kinds of requirements that set a minimum on the amount of reserves a bank has to keep on hand. The legal minimum is set by the banking regulators. In the US, demand deposits require a 10% reserve to be kept on hand, and time deposits require zero, though there are exemptions that complicate it. The other kind of minimum is the practical one: a bank has to keep enough on hand to avoid running out of money. A bank has to maintain whichever minimum is larger. (19)

**reserves**   Money a bank has to keep around as cash and equivalent to satisfy their customers' withdrawals. Since many withdrawals will actually be from one bank to another, much of this money can be held as reserves, at the Federal Reserve bank (now you understand the name?), where it can be readily transferred from bank to bank. (18)

**retail bank**   A bank that serves ordinary people and businesses as its customers. Also known as a commercial bank. (71)

**retained profit**   Part of capital, this is money that could have been distributed to shareholders but wasn't, and was reinvested in the bank instead. (18)

**revenue bond**   A government bond backed not by the full credit of some government, but by some specific revenue stream that has been identified for that bond. For example, a bond to extend a sewer line might be restricted to be repaid by the fees paid by the new users of the sewer. Of course if the promised revenue doesn't materialize, you'll hear bond owners talking about how the bond is a "moral obligation" even if it's not a legal one. (132)

**risk model**   A set of assumptions and guesses about how markets work gussied up in a lot of impenetrable statistics to acquire an air of authority. A risk model is supposed to predict likely changes in value of the assets a bank owns and to estimate worst-case scenarios. What's usually omitted from these calculations is that an event with a 1-in-1000 chance of happening on any given day usually does happen every three years, just because 3 years is more than a thousand days. (94)

**RP**   See "repo transaction." (64)

**RTGS**   A Real-Time Gross Settlement system is a system of payments where the transfer of funds is instantaneous. These are usually used for very large transactions, since they tend to be expensive individually. (77)

**RWA**   The sum of the asset values, multiplied by "weights" that are an estimate of how risky the asset is. Zero-risk assets get a zero weight, and very risky assets get a weight of 100% or greater. A 100% weight means the entire value of the asset class is at risk. This is the asset value that goes into a CRAR calculation. (27)

# S

**seasonal credit**   One of the categories of credit available to banks through the Federal Reserve's "discount window." Seasonal credit is for longer terms than primary or secondary credit, and was originally intended to make loans to banks with a lot of agricultural lending, which tends to be repaid at harvest time. (64)

**SEC**   The Securities and Exchange Commission regulates the stock market, to the extent anyone does, and has a broad portfolio of other regulatory responsibilities in the financial industry. (89)

**secondary credit**   A category of credit available through the Fed's "discount window." Secondary credit is for slightly worse credit risks than primary credit, so has a higher interest rate, but is otherwise about the same. (64)

**securitization**   The packaging of some asset, like a set of loans, or anything that produces some income, into a bond. Investors purchase the bond and receive the right to that income. (56)

**shadow bank**   A financial institution that is not a bank, but is engaged in what amount to banking activities. For example, a money market fund that takes short-term funding from its shareholders and makes long-term investments in mortgages is engaged in classic bank activities. A student loan agency funded by bonds is doing something similar. Both of these are behaving like banks, and have customers who behave like bank customers, but their activities are not regulated by bank regulators. Note, of course, that the money market fund is probably making those mortgage investments through bonds issued by some bank's off-balance sheet SIV. That is, it may not be a truly independent entity. (101)

**share account**   The form of membership in a credit union. Members will have a share account, along with whatever other accounts at the credit union they need. (146)

**SIV**   A Special Interest Vehicle is a corporate entity constructed to shift assets or liabilities off a corporation's balance sheet. The idea is to create a corporation (the SIV) to do with those assets (or liabilities) exactly what the parent company would have done with them, but in such a way that the parent company doesn't actually "own" them or the SIV, at least in an accounting sense. This might be because the SIV's owners include other parties, or it might be because risk models have "determined" that someone else will be on the hook for any losses (so the ownership need not be acknowledged on the balance sheet), or they might just be lying. Either way, the parent company no longer has to account for the SIV's assets or liabilities (or risks) on their books. (99)

**SOSD**    Alan Greenspan's "state of shocked disbelief" that banks would not regulate themselves. Not widely shared among free marketeers, among whom there has been a marked lack of humility even among the wreckage of the nation's economy caused by the banking binge of 2000–2007. (87)

**SPE**    A Special Purpose Entity, see "SIV." (99)

**swaption**    An option to make a swap agreement at some time in the future. You might sell me an option to enter into a swap with me next week, in which case I pay you some money and next week I get to decide whether to enter into the swap or not. If at that point you don't want to make a swap, you will usually have to pay me a penalty or withdrawal fee. (138)

**swipe fee**    A fee paid by a merchant for each credit card transaction they process. Merchants in the US pay very high swipe fees compared to other countries. (45)

**synthetic lease**    A lease between a corporation and some subsidiary it has invented just to have someone to make lease payments to. For example, the Acme Explosives Company could create a subsidiary to own the trademark "AEC" and lease the trademark back from the subsidiary. This sounds dopey, but it is a standard way to move profits from one taxing jurisdiction to another as you could see if Acme's subsidiary was incorporated in the Cayman Islands. (99)

# T

**T-bill**    A US treasury bond with a maturity of less than a year. Bonds with one- to five-year maturity are "notes" and the rest are just "bonds." (55)

**TAN**    A Tax Anticipation Note is a government-issued short-term bond. The government in question is borrowing against taxes it expects to get in the next few months, sometimes longer. In earlier, more innocent time, revenue ebbs and flows would be dealt with by keeping a substantial cash reserve in the bank. In the modern, professionalized, financialized, world, we can borrow from bankers to cover those shortfalls, paying bond counsel and underwriters for what used to be just a bank withdrawal. Ah, progress. (55)

**tax increment financing**   See "TIF." (133)

**thrift**   A kind of bank intended to serve consumers rather than businesses, sometimes called a "Savings and Loan." The idea was to have an institution meant to do mortgages and car loans for families. George Bailey's bank was a thrift, contrasted with Mr. Potter's commercial bank across the street. In modern reality, the distinction between the two types of banks has eroded and it's difficult to tell the difference any more. (9)

**Tier 1 capital**   A measurement of the amount of money a bank can afford to lose before it starts losing customer deposits. Roughly equal to the value of the bank stock, plus the retained profits, minus the intangible assets. (25)

**Tier 2 capital**   Money a bank has, but has already dedicated to losses. A loan loss allowance is an example of Tier 2 capital. (25)

**TIF**   A "tax increment financing" bond is sort of like a revenue bond except that repayment of the bond is supposed to come from new tax revenue attributable to the project the bond will finance. For example, a bond to build a new park might be repaid by the increase in property tax collections due to increased property values around the park. There are a lot of ways to write a TIF, some of which will help a city and some of which are only intended to exploit a city. (133)

**time deposits**   A deposit with a term. You put your money in the bank and get it out at the agreed-upon time. A CD is a time deposit. Contrast with a "demand deposit." (19)

**trading account**   A bank's trading account consists of investments the bank has made on its own behalf. This is supposedly money that belongs to the bank, and not to its customers. Money is fungible, so this is a distinction that is often meaningless. But there's profit involved, so banks try to perpetuate the distinction since it gives them a freer hand. (33)

**tranche**   A bond with income derived from many debts can be subdivided. A mortgage-backed bond can have two or more "tranches" with different claims on the income from the underlying mortgages. (The word is French for "slice.") A "senior" tranche might have the first claim on income up to half the predicted amount, and the junior tranche on whatever income is left after that. The different claims entail different risks, and therefore different bond ratings, different prices, and different interest rates. (135)

**trust**   An independent corporate entity with some assets to manage, not owned by anyone. (43)

# U

**UAAL**   The Unfunded Actuarially Accrued Liability is the difference between the value of a pension fund's assets and the present value of its future liabilities. It is a less meaningful number than the "funding ratio" but will usually sound more impressive, since it doesn't require a huge government to have billions in unfunded liabilities. (125)

**UBHPR**   A UBPR for bank holding companies. (91)

**UBPR**   The Uniform Bank Performance Reports are available at the FFIEC web site, and contain most of the information from a bank's quarterly "call report." (91)

**unfunded liability**   See "UAAL." (125)

# V

**VA**   The Veterans Administration is the other big mortgage-insuring federal agency, after the FHA. (58)

**VaR**   The Value at Risk is an estimate of how much asset value is at risk of being lost on a terrible day at the races. It is essentially the output of a bank's risk models. It is, of course, subject to a number of assumptions about probability, the markets, and the weather, so any particular VaR measurement should be taken with at least a grain of salt. (94)

**venture capital fund**  A private equity fund aimed at finding and investing in startup businesses. Usually the last resort of startup businesses who need capital, since VC funds usually come with lots of strings, including a loss of ownership. (74)

# W

**wholesale bank**  See "banker's bank." (71)

**wire transfer**  An immediate transfer of funds from one financial institution to another. There is no clearing or netting done with a wire transfer. (77)

# Y

**yield to maturity**  The money earned by a bond, expressed as a percentage of the bond price. The actual yield calculation is pretty complicated, so the "current yield" is often used as a decent approximation. (129)

# Z

**zero-balance account**  A transaction account into which money is automatically shifted as needed, to maintain a balance of zero. This is meant to maximize the amount of money in a companion savings or investment account. (128)

**zero-coupon bond**  A bond that only makes one payment, the repayment of the principal and all the interest, at the end of the term. Usually sold with a face value equal to the final payout amount, and bought at a discount from that value. (129)

# Index

**#**
100% reserve banking, 40
3-6-3 business, 42
95% confidence
    don't trust, 95

**A**
AAA rating
    did not deserve, 136
account
    zero-balance, 127
accounting
    capital, 18
    creative, 21
    debate, 101, 125
    equation, 15
    fossil, 32
    fraud, 45
    pension, 125
    risk weighting, 27
accredited investors, 74
ACH, 78
Acme Credit Union, 60
    managing reserves, 62
acquiring bank, 78
activist
    dilettante, 1
actuarially required contribution, 126
advances, 69

Aeneid, 137
aggression
    in executive suite, 63
airline
    shedding risk, 48
Akerlof, George, 103
alliance of towns
    public bank, 155
allowance
    loan loss, 23, 33
Alt-A, 5
apologia, 1
arbitrage, 42
ARC, 126
Archimedes, 36
Asia
    public bank, 147
ask price, 131
assessment, 93
asset statement, 123
asset-backed bond, 56
assets, 16
    cash, 30
    includes buildings, 21
    intangible, 22, 110
    loan loss allowance, 23, 33
    reserves, 18
    surplus, 22
    under management, 98

asymmetrical information, 103
ATM, 80
audit requirements
    government, 127
AUM, 98
authority
    government component,
        119
authorization
    credit card, 78
automated clearing house, 78

**B**
balance sheet, 15
    asset statement, 123
    examples, 31
    lending, 50
    loan loss allowance, 23,
        33
    projections, 114
    Sunnydale example, 19
Bancorp, 108
bank
    banker's, 71
    block diagram, 41
    borrowing, 58
    business plan, 110
    card, 78
    charter, 107
    community, 52
    correspondent, 30
    draft, 76
    failure, 93
    fee income, 42
    government customers,
        117
    holy grail, 66
    income, 42
    investment, 72
    Islamic, 39
    lending from float, 108

making money, 50
managing capital, 25
morality, 39
municipal bond, 135
mutual, 146
non-bank, 101
North Dakota, 32
overhead, 59
plan, 106
private-label, 71, 111
public, 32
public funds, 117
Rhode Island crisis, 1, 47
risk weighting assets, 27
run, 93
shadow, 101
shedding risk, 11
starting Sunnydale, 22
starting up, 105
stock, 35
stock as capital, 17
surplus, 35
surplus capital, 22
vendors, 111
wholesale, 71
bank charter
    choosing, 107
bank equity capital, 18
bank fee
    letter of credit, 139
Bank for International Settle-
        ments, 81, 88
Bank of America
    accounting, 21
    balance sheet, 31
    brokered deposits, 61
    founding, 161
    padding bond sales, 141
Bank of England, 81
Bank of Italy, 161
Bank of North Dakota, 32

balance sheet, 32
  moving beyond, 149
  surplus, 36
  wholesale bank, 71
bank run, 46
banker's bank, 71
bankruptcy
  FDIC supervised, 93
Basel Accords, 25
basis points, 49
beans, magic, 83
Beckman, C. E., 75
Bedford Falls, 6
Bernanke, Ben, 7
Bible
  prohibition of usury, 39
bid price, 131
BIS, 81, 88
bitcoin, 82
BND, see Bank of North Dakota
bond, 53
  asset-backed, 56
  capital appreciation, 140
  churning, 138
  commercial paper, 55
  counsel, 131
  coupon, 129
  debenture, 131
  flipping, 141
  general obligation, 132
  insurance, 135
  issuer, 128
  managing proceeds, 131
  moral obligation, 132
  mortgage-backed, 56
  municipal bank, 135
  mutual insurer, 144
  OTC transactions, 72
  padding sales, 141
  payment system, 80
  pension obligation, 139

price, 134
pricing, 128
private placement, 54
rating, 134
refi, see refunding
refunding, 133
revenue, 132
short-term, see note
tax anticipation, 128, 142
third-party, 132
TIF, 133
tranche, 135
trustee, 131
underwriter, 43, 54, 130
yield, 134
zero-coupon, 128
bond dealer
  investment bank, 72
bond market
  FHLB, 69
  investment banks, 72
  pressure on banks, 54
borrowing
  bond market, 53, 66
  from other banks, 67
  government plans, 122
  money market, 65
branch
  cost of, 59
brokered deposits, 61
budget document, 120
  capital planning, 122
budget reserve, 122
Build America Mutual, 144
bus ticket
  risk, 48
business plan, 110
Business Plan Guidelines
  OTS, 112
business-type activities, 119
buy-back agreement, 39

## C

CAFR, 123
  notes best part, 124
call provision, 129
call report, 91
capital, 17
  backdating with OTS, 19
  leverage, 37
  mobility, 81
  mutual bank, 17
  practical reality, 25
  startup, 109
  surplus, 22, 35
capital adequacy ratio, 24
capital appreciation bond, 140
capital planning documents, 122
capital risk
  vs. asset risk, 28
CAR, 24
carpets, assets, 16
cash
  asset of bank, 30
  supplied by Fed, 68
cash manager, 128
cash reserve, 122
CD, 19
CDARS, 127
CDFI, 151
CDO, 56
cell phone payments, 82
CFPB, 91
  conception, 161
CFTC, 90
charter
  necessary, 107
check, 76
  clearing, 50, 76
  electronic, 77
  security features, 76
check-cashing store, 154

China
  public bank, 147
CHIPS, 77
churning
  bond, 138
Citigroup
  bond churning, 138
  brokered deposits, 61
  padding bond sales, 141
  Philadelphia swaps deal, 6
Citizens Bank
  balance sheet, 31
clearing, 76
clearing house, 76
  ACH, 77
  CHIPS, 77
Clearing House Interbank Payment System, 77
closed-end investment company, 73
coins, 68
collateral, deposit, 126
collateralized debt obligation, 56
commercial paper, 55
Commodity Futures Trading Commission, 90
community banks, 53
community development financial institution, 151
Community Reinvestment Act, 91
comprehensive annual financial report, 123
concentration risk, 47
Connecticut
  pension bond, 139
  sued bond raters, 118
Consumer Financial Protection Bureau, 91

Cordray, Richard, 91
correspondent accounts, 70
correspondent banks, 30
cost of funds, 17, 59
Countrywide Financial, 5, 88
coupon bond, 129
coupon rate, 129
CRA, 91
    OTS rule of thumb, 92
CRAR, 28
credit
    emergency, 64, 72
    letter of, 43, 139
    primary, 63
    rating agencies, 134
    risk, 45
    seasonal, 63
    secondary, 63
credit card, 78
    association, 78
    fees, 44
    usury, 79
credit default swap, 65
credit rating agency, 134
credit risk, 24
credit union, 145
    Acme, 60
current yield, 129
CUSIP number, 130

**D**
de novo, 52
debenture, 131
debit card, 79
    pre-pay, 79
debt
    hiding, 140
demand deposits, 19, 59
democratization of finance
    risks, 10

Depository Trust & Clearing
    Corporation, 80
deposits
    attracting, 51
    brokered, 61
    cost of, 59
    insurance, 93
    managing, 59
deregulation
    interest rate, 65
    risk of, 10
derivative contract
    priority, 93
dilettante
    activists, 1
Dimon, Jamie, 63
disbelief
    state of shocked, *see* SOSD
discount rate, 64
    pension, 125
discount window, 63
Dodd-Frank, 43, 91
draft, 76
DTCC, 80

**E**
earnings
    not retained, 36
    retained, 18
electronic check, 77
electronic payments, 77
emergency credit, 64, 72
Enron, 99
enterprise fund, 119
Epstein, Abe, 161
equation
    accounting, 15
equity, 17
exchange, 90
excluded middle, 16

## F

face value
  bond, 129
Fannie Mae, 56
FASB, 15, 89
FDIC, 92
  receiver, 93
  regulatory guidelines, 29
Fed, 20, 68
Fed funds, 32, 62
  managing with, 62
  not private, 64
  purchased, 34
  rate, 68
  sold, 32
Federal Deposit Insurance Corporation, 92
Federal Financial Institutions
  Examination Coun-
  cil, 90
Federal Home Loan Bank, 69
Federal Housing Administration, 58
Federal Reserve, *see* Fed
Fedwire, 77
fee income, 42
  credit cards, 44
FFIEC, 90
FHA, 58
FHLB, 69
finance
  government, 117
Financial Accounting Standards
  Board, 15, 89
financial advisor, 131
financial capital, 24
financial industry
  abetted industrial collapse,
  148
  vendors, 111

Financial Industry Regulatory
  Authority, 89
financial network, 67
financial projection
  balancing, 115
  creating, 113
financial reform
  by replacement, 105
financial report
  comprehensive, 123
financial services
  for the poor, 154
FINRA, 89
Fitch, 134
flipping bonds, 141
float, lending from, 108
fractional reserve banking, 38
fraud
  accounting, 45
Freddie Mac, 56
Fuld, Richard, 63
full reserve banking, 40
fund balance, 123
funding ratio, 125
funds
  cost of, 17

## G

GAAP, 89
GASB, 89, 123
general fund, 121
general obligation bond, 132
Germany
  public bank, 147
Giannini, Amadeo, 161
Ginnie Mae, 56
Glass-Steagall, 43
Goldman Sachs
  brokered deposits, 61
  commodities, 90
  padding bond sales, 141

Philadelphia swaps deal,
    6
government
    audit requirements, 127
    authority, 119
    borrowing bonds, 53
    borrowing plans, 122
    budget, 120
    components, 119
    financial reform, 148
government finance, 117
government-sponsored enter-
    prises, 56
Governmental Accounting Stan-
    dards Board, 89
grail, holy, 66
Greenspan, Alan
    SOSD, 87
Gresham's Law, 57
GSE, 56

H
health insurance
    risk, 48
hedge fund, 74
Heritage S&L, 47
heteroskedasticity, 95
hiding risk, 98
Hogg, Tom, 165
holding company, 108
holy grail
    interest swap, 66

I
IFRS, 101
income statement, 22
    P&L statement, 123
    projections, 114
income, types of, 42
industrial collapse
    finance, 148

IndyMac, 5, 61, 88
information asymmetry, 103
insider jargon, 18
instant e-payment, 77
insurance
    deposit, 93
    loan, 58
intangible assets, 22, 110
interchange fee, 44
interest rate
    bond, 66
    deregulation, 10, 65
    Fed discount, 63
    Fed funds, 68
    no limits, 79
    pension, 125
    Philadelphia swap, 6
    repo, 64
    risk, 46, 85
    swap, 65
    swap for fixed, 65
internal service fund, 119
International Financial Report-
    ing Standards, 101
international payments
    CHIPS, 77
interstate banking
    growth and risk, 11
inversely correlated, 94
investment bank, 72
investment company, 72
Islamic banking, 39
issuer, 129
issuing bank, 78
It's a Wonderful Life, 6

J
jargon
    in-group badge, 18
JPMorgan
    commodities, 90

netting use, 101
off-balance sheet, 101
padding bond sales, 141
trading account, 33, 34

**L**
laddered investments, 151
laundering money, 70
lease
operating, 98
Lehman Brothers, 7
repercussions, 73
tranche risk, 136
Lemons, Market for, 103
lending
balance sheet, 50
doesn't scale, 52
loan insurance, 58
money market, 54, 65
participation, 70
secondary market, 43, 56
syndicate, 70
takes time, 51
letter of credit, 43
Port of Oakland, 139
leverage, 36
and risk, 38
Lehman Brothers, 7
off-balance sheet, 101
reduced by netting, 101
leverage ratio, 37
Lewis, Kenneth, 63
liability, 17
pension, 125
liar loans, 5
LIBOR, 142
rigging, 142
lifeboat example, 137
liquidity risk, 20, 46
loan loss allowance, 23, 33
fudge for profit, 45

loan loss reserve, 33
loan to deposit ratio, 34
LOC, see letter of credit
lockbox service, 44, 77
Louisiana
bond churning, 138
Luna, Miguel, 165
lunch
industrial, eaten, 148

**M**
magic beans, 50, 83
managing
bond proceeds, 131
deposits, 59
lending, 51
reserves, 61, 62
risk by shedding, 96
market maker, 131
market risk, 46
maturity transformation, 40
MBS, see mortgage-backed bond
ignorant buyer, 103
mobility of capital
comparable to 1800's, 81
modeling
assumptions, 94
risk, 94
Mollicone, Joe
embezzlement record, 47
money
bitcoin, 82
cost of, 17
creation, 83
creation conundrum, 77
laundering, 70
making it up, 50
moving, 75
physical object, 81
requires banks, 11
money market, 55, 59

fund, 73
Moody's, 134
moral obligation, 133
morality
    bank, 39
Morgan Stanley
    brokered deposits, 61
    padding bond sales, 141
    Philadelphia swaps deal,
        6
mortgage
    insurance, 58
    liquidity via FHLB, 69
mortgage-backed bond, 56
mortgagee, 69
mortgagor, 69
Mozilo, Angelo, 63
MSRB, 90
multiplier, 84
municipal bond bank, 135
municipal bonds, 130
Municipal Securities Rulemak-
        ing Board, 90
mutual bank, 146
    capital, 17
    FHLB, 69
mutual fund, 73
mutual insurance
    bond, 144

**N**

NASD, 89
NASDAQ, 89
National Association of Se-
        curities Dealers, 89
National Housing Act of 1934,
        56
National Settlement Service,
        76
NCUA, 93
net assets, 123

netting, 101
    off-balance sheet, 101
netting e-payment, 77
netting engine, 77
New Bedford, 75
New Deal legacy, 56, 69, 89,
        92
New York Stock Exchange,
        89
NINJA, 104
no-doc, 104
non-bank banks, 102
North Dakota
    bank of, 32
    moving beyond, 149
Northampton County
    swaption deal, 138
note, 55
    commercial paper, 55
    tax anticipation, 55, 128,
        142
    Treasury, 55
notes
    CAFR highlights, 124
NSS, 76
NYSE, 89

**O**

OCC, 88
Occupy Money, 160
off-balance sheet, 98
    JPMorgan, 101
    lease, 98
    Lehman Brothers, 7, 101
    netting, 101
    shadow banking, 102
    State Street Bank, 100
Office of the Comptroller of
        the Currency, 88
Office of Thrift Supervision,
        88

Old Stone Bank, 47
OPEB, 125
open ended investment com-
	pany, 73
open market operations, 68
open repo, 64
operating lease, 98
operational risk, 47
originate-and-distribute, 96
OTC, 72, 90
other post-employment ben-
	efit, 125
OTS, 5, 88
	backdating capital, 19
	Business Plan Guidelines,
		112
	CRA rule of thumb, 92
	shame of, 88
outsourcing
	advantages of, 111
over the counter, 72, 90
own account, *see* trading ac-
	count

**P**
P&L, 22
PACE loans, 58
padding bond sales, 141
Pan Am, 99
par value, 35, 129
participation lending, 71
Pasadena
	not like Bedford Falls, 6
Paulson, Henry, 7
payday lender, 154
payment processing
	bank income, 44
payment system, 75
	bitcoin, 82
	bonds, 80
	cell phone minutes, 82

check, 76
electronic, 77
security, 75, 76
pension
	fund, 125
	obligation bond, 139
pension fund
	bond investors, 53
Philadelphia
	first mutual bank, 147
	interest rate swap, 6, 66,
		137
plan
	business, 110
pledged deposits, 146
PMI, 58
point-of-sale terminal, 80
poker chips
	limit of analogy, 24
POS, 80
positive pay, 76
Postal Service, 126
Poway school
	capital appreciation bond,
		140
pre-pay debit card, 79
predatory public finance, 137
	bond churning, 138
	bond flipping, 141
	capital appreciation bond,
		140
	interest rate swap, 66
	LIBOR rigging, 142
	padding bond sales, 141
	pension obligation bond,
		139
	tax anticipation note, 142
present value, 125
price banking, 11
pricing bonds, 128
primary credit, 63

private equity fund, 74
private jets, assets, 16
private placement, 54
private-label bank, 71, 111
profit
 bond sales, 43
 not retained, 36
 retained, 18, 36
profit-and-loss, 22
projections
 creating financial, 113
Property Assessed Clean Energy, 58
proprietary funds, 119
public bank
 alliance of towns, 155
 assemblage of parts, 156
 balance sheet, 32
 CDFI amplifier, 151
 China, Germany, 147
 North Dakota, 147
 service bureau, 152
 serving the unbanked, 155
 startup predictable, 148
 surplus, 36
public finance
 predatory, 137
public funds, 117
public funds, collateral, 126
purpose for bank, 106

**Q**
quantum mechanics, 83

**R**
Raines, Franklin, 63
rainy day fund, 122
RAN, *see* TAN
rating agencies, 134
 Connecticut sued, 118
 shame of, 103, 136

Reading, PA, 160
real-time gross settlement, 77
receivership, 93
redlining, 91
refinance, bond, *see* refunding
refunding, 133
regulators, 88
 BIS, 88
 CFPB, 91
 CFTC, 90
 CRA, 91
 FASB, 89
 FDIC, 29, 88, 92
 Fed, 88
 FFIEC, 90
 FHA, 89
 FINRA, 89
 GASB, 89
 make friends with, 113
 MSRB, 90
 NCUA, 88, 93
 OCC, 88
 SEC, 89
 shame of, 5, 19, 21, 35,
  36, 44, 47, 61, 88, 90
regulatory risk, 47
relationship banking, 11
repo, 32, 34, 64
repo rate, 64
repurchase agreement, 32, 64
reserve
 budget, 121
 cash, 122
Reserve Primary, 73
reserves, 18
 effect of increasing, 20
 Fed funds market, 62
 fractional, 38
 increasing, 51
 loan loss, 33

managing, 61
minimum, 60
requirement, 19
Sunnydale example, 19
restricted funds, government,
       121
retail bank, 71
retained earnings, 18
retained profit, 18, 36
revenue anticipation note, *see*
       tax anticipation note
revenue bond, 132
reverse repo, 32
Rhode Island
     bank crisis, 1, 47
     must borrow, 143
     Old Stone Bank, 47
     risk aversion, 150
rigging
     LIBOR, 142
risk
     aversion, 150
     capital vs. assets, 28
     concentration, 47
     credit, 45
     finding suckers, 11, 48
     hedging, 137
     hiding, 98
     interest rate, 46, 85
     interstate banking, 11
     leverage, 36, 38
     liquidity, 46
     manage by shedding, 8,
         11, 96
     market, 46
     modeling, 94
     off-balance sheet, 100
     operational, 47
     popular reforms, 10
     regulatory, 47
     shedding is systemic, 97

SIVs, 98
tornadoes, 47
types of, 45
weighting assets, 27
risk-weighted assets, 27
RP, 64
RTGS, 77
run, bank, 46
RWA, 27

S

San Diego
     capital appreciation bond,
         140
     tax anticipation note, 142
Sarbanes-Oxley, 100
school district
     Philadelphia, 6
Schumer, Senator Chuck, 5
seasonal credit, 64
SEC, 89
secondary credit, 63
secondary market, 43
     and risk, 97
securities
     asset of bank, 30
Securities and Exchange Com-
         mission, 89
securitization, 56
self-regulation, *see* SOSD
shadow banks, 40, 102
     bank cats-paw, 102
share account, 146
shedding risk
     instead of managing, 11,
         96
     not managing, 8
shell corporation, 99
shocked disbelief, *see* SOSD
Simple.com, 112
SIV, 99

Skilling, Jeffrey, 99
Social Security
    conception, 161
SOSD, 87, 90, 96, 105
SPE, 99
special interest vehicle, 99
special purpose entity, 99
Spiderman, 150
spread, 131
spreadsheet
    financial projection, 113
Standard & Poor's, 134
starting a bank
    holding company, 108
    kind of charter, 107
startup capital
    how used, 109
State Street Bank
    off-balance sheet, 100
statement of net assets, 123
subprime mortgages
    AAA bonds, 28
    Lehman Brothers, 7
    market risk, 46
suckers, finding, 48
Sunnydale
    balance sheet, 19
    better example, 26
    origin story, 22
surplus capital, 22, 35
swap, 65
    interest rate, 65
swaption, 138
    Northampton County, 138
swipe fee, 44
syndicate, 70
synthetic lease, 99

**T**

T-bill, 55
    without risk, 28

TAN, *see* tax anticipation note
tax anticipation note, 55, 128,
    142
tax increment financing, 133
term deposits, 59
thrift, 5
    federal charter, 107
Tier 1 capital, 25
Tier 2 capital, 25
TIF, 133
time deposits, 19
toasters, 41
tornado
    operational risk, 47
trading account, 33, 34
tranche
    bond, 135
    risk of, 136
transaction accounts, 19
Treasury bill, 55
Trippe, Juan, 99
trust, 43
trustee
    bond, 131

**U**

UAAL, 125
UBHPR, 91
UBPR, 91
underwriter, 43, 54, 130
underwriter's counsel, 131
unfunded liability, 125
Uniform Bank Performance
    Reports, 91
usury
    credit cards, 79
    ecclesiastic prohibition, 39

**V**

VA, 58
value at risk, 94

VaR, 94
vendors, financial industry,
       111
venture capital fund, 74
Vermont
       mortgage broker, 144
Veterans Administration, 58
volatility, deposits, 60

**W**
Warren, Elizabeth, 91, 161
Washington Mutual, 88
Washington Trust
       balance sheet, 31
Wells Fargo
       Philadelphia swaps deal,
       6
wholesale bank, 71
wire transfer, 77

**Y**
yield, 129

**Z**
zero-balance account, 128
zero-coupon bond, 129
       capital appreciation, 140

## Want to hear more?

The author is available to speak at your event.

"Tom gave a workshop about banking nuts and bolts at the Public Banking Institute's 2013 conference and it was superb—clear and to the point, and a pleasure to attend. It was the best-attended workshop of the conference. Tom's contributions and ideas are well developed and foundational—he is PBI's 'go-to' person for any questions concerning public finance."

*Marc Armstrong, Executive Director, Public Banking Institute (publicbankinginstitute.org)*

"Tom Sgouros was an irreplaceable part of our conference. His knowledge about banking and finance is clearly extensive. His talk was thought-provoking, well organized, and dynamically delivered. He had the audience captivated from the moment he popped a podium out of his briefcase to the closing words of his speech."

*Matt Feinstein, media and organizing coordinator, Worcester Roots Co-op Project (worcesterroots.org)*

Please find contact information on the copyright page.

CPSIA information can be obtained at www.ICGtesting.com
Printed in the USA
LVOW11s1546240214

374966LV00001B/357/P